'I loved this book! Nikki's writing is as powerful as her spoken word. Her practical advice, coupled with personal experience, is applicable to everyone – even the busiest professional juggling disruption on multiple levels. This book is a must-read for anyone dealing with disruption or loss on any scale.'

– Dharshni Padayachee, Inclusion, Diversity and Transformation Lead, Rand Merchant Bank

'These turbulent times, which are in part due to the catalytic effect of the global pandemic, are radically altering what we do and how we do it. Conceptually, we know we need to adapt and future-proof ourselves against these seismic changes. But we just don't know how. Nikki has authored a brilliant, practical blueprint on how to do just that.'

– Siphiwe Moyo, global speaker and adjunct faculty member at GIBS, Henley and Wits Business Schools

'Nikki's wisdom and heartfelt experience shine in this brilliant book. There is no one better to be your guide through disruption and change.'

– Caspar Craven, speaker and author of *Be More Human: Rethinking the Rules of High-Performance Teamwork* (Starting Point, 2020)

'Nikki Bush turns the patronising and destructive practice of rescuing people – at home, school and work – on its head, substituting empowerment and accountability instead, helping readers to become future-fit.'

– Dereck Jackson, veteran educator and psychologist

'Nikki Bush has created a timely and essential guide to navigating the disruption that comes from unplanned change in both our personal and professional lives.' **– Madeleine Black, author of *Unbroken: One Woman's Journey to Rebuild a Life Shattered by Violence* (John Blake, 2017)**

'An insightful book that allows us the space to reflect on the adaptations required to prepare for the decade to come, both personally and in the workplace, to face a new world head-on.'

– Kenda Melvill-Smith, Head, St Peter's Boys Prep School

'This is no textbook. Nikki writes from a powerful place of personal experience. She shows vulnerability, her strength of character and the courage needed to heal, reinvent and rediscover through change and loss. Nikki is proof that our mission in life is to find our gift, and our purpose is to give it away.'

– Margaret Hirsch, women's empowerment champion and winner of the Most Influential Women in Business in Africa award

'Nikki has penned a practical book that presents in progressive flow an intertwined thread of her disruptive trauma. What I found extremely useful was the powerful juxtaposition of collateral damage and collateral beauty as an exercise that can evoke gratitude and appreciation, and enable you to win at work, home and life. No doubt a must-read!'

– Dr Alex Granger, ThinkShifter, global speaker, author and executive coach

'A must-read for everyone, as we constantly dance with disruption and change. Nikki writes the way she speaks – with warmth, sincerity and depth. I couldn't put it down. We can all learn from Nikki's story and insights.'

– Glynne Wolman, founder of The Angel Network

While juggling the many balls of being a wife, mom, business owner, international speaker, coach and board member, I often wonder how others like me handle the pressures of life. It's like Nikki read my mind! This incredible read (which straddles between practical handbook and inspirational message) is exactly what I've been looking for. Nikki's approach is so relaxed, realistic and packed with practical wisdom.

– Deshun Deysel, CEO of Go Peak International Pty (Ltd) and pioneering African female mountaineer

May your curiosity always be stronger than your fear! Nikki Bush

FUTURE-PROOF YOURSELF

How to win at work and life

NIKKI BUSH

PENGUIN BOOKS

Future-proof Yourself
Published by Penguin Books
an imprint of Penguin Random House South Africa (Pty) Ltd
Reg. No. 1953/000441/07
The Estuaries No. 4, Oxbow Crescent, Century Avenue, Century City, 7441
PO Box 1144, Cape Town, 8000, South Africa
www.penguinrandomhouse.co.za

PENGUIN BOOKS

First published 2021

1 3 5 7 9 10 8 6 4 2

PUBLISHER: Marlene Fryer
MANAGING EDITOR: Ronel Richter-Herbert
EDITOR: Christa Büttner-Rohwer
PROOFREADER: Alice Inggs
COVER AND TEXT DESIGNER: Ryan Africa
TYPESETTER: Monique Cleghorn

Set in 11 pt on 15 pt Minion

Printed by **novus print**, a division of Novus Holdings

Penguin Random House is committed to
a sustainable future for our business, our readers
and our planet. This book is made from Forest
Stewardship Council® certified paper.

ISBN 978 177609 588 9 (print)
ISBN 978 177609 589 6 (ePub)

MIX
Paper from
responsible sources
FSC® C022948
FSC
www.fsc.org

In loving memory of Simon Bush, my husband of twenty-six years, amazing dad to our two boys, and memorable friend to many. You were a 6'5" gentle giant in life. We miss your gentleness, your dignity, your respect for others, your wicked sense of humour and that mischievous sparkle in your eyes. You left indelible footprints in our hearts and minds. You were an enabler of my voice in life, just as you are in death. Your impact continues.

CONTENTS

ABOUT THIS BOOK

When last did you get lost? I mean, really lost. A moment when you had absolutely no idea where you were going or how to get to where you were supposed to be. This experience rarely happens in our lives these days because we live in an era of Google Maps and Waze – satellite navigation systems you can depend on (as long as you have connectivity). In fact, I bet you hadn't felt truly lost for very a long time until the global coronavirus pandemic hit. Once the initial shock of disbelief started to dissipate, it began to feel like you were caught in a swirling white-out, didn't it? Lost, fearful and out of control, with no view of the future. No sense of certainty.

At 9 p.m. one night, a week before the beginning of the Covid-19 lockdown, I was driving between Pietermaritzburg and the little town of Hilton in KwaZulu-Natal after giving an evening presentation. I typed the address of my B&B into Waze on my cellphone and set off, not giving it a second thought. I trusted Waze to do what it was supposed to do: take me to my B&B via the fastest and most direct route. This happened to be up the old road and not on the motorway.

As I live in Johannesburg, the last thing on my mind was mist – a regular occurrence in that hilly part of South Africa that I hadn't visited for some years. I was only a few kilometres up the hill before I became engulfed in a thick bank of fog, unable to see the road ahead, let alone behind me or to either side. I decided it would be safer to pull over and stop with my car's hazard lights on. There was no way I could continue, as I was unfamiliar with the roads in the area.

A couple of minutes later a car pulled up in front of me, also with its hazards on. As the driver got out, I recognised her as the organiser of the event at which I had just spoken. She didn't usually drive this road because of the mist, but here she was, sent to guide me. I cannot tell you how relieved I was to have someone to follow. I would never have found my way home without her.

As we pulled away, driving between twenty and thirty kilometres per hour, a huge lump caught in my throat and I started to cry – hard, wracking, uncontrollable sobs. My face was wet with tears and I only had one soggy tissue. I could barely see for the tears, never mind the mist!

Driving into that wall of white, not knowing what was in front of me, had triggered feelings from two years earlier, when my family and I had been brutally attacked in our home by armed intruders at 3 a.m. on a Saturday morning. I had managed to lock myself in the bathroom while we were under siege. In that moment, as I found myself on the bathroom floor, wedged between the laundry basket and the toilet, making six emergency calls on my cellphone, I felt caught in a thick mist of utter uncertainty: How many intruders were on our property? Where were they? What were they doing to my husband and my eighteen-year-old son? What would they do to me? And how would this end? I felt lost, frightened, and completely out of control. Exactly the same feelings came over me as the mist overwhelmed me on the road up to Hilton. Perhaps you too can identify with these feelings as we live through a time of great uncertainty.

You'll never know what the future holds until you emerge through the mist or open the door you dread opening. As I drove to Hilton, I knew that warmth and comfort awaited me at my B&B. But on that fateful night two years earlier I had no idea what would await me when I opened the bathroom door. I found that my husband had been murdered – a discovery that led to the greatest disruption of my life.

This book is not about Covid-19. Nor is it the full story of the six minutes that changed my life. However, I will draw on these experiences and some of the lessons and frameworks I have distilled from them to help you to cope with disruption of any kind. We will also look at some of the steps you can take to future-proof yourself, no matter what life throws at you, so that you can continue to win at work and life.

The pandemic has been a stark reminder for everyone that life doesn't unfold in a straight line. We have to learn how to better respond to and prepare ourselves for the unexpected – emotionally and practically.

My approach to disruption is very different to that of most people. I look at it through the eyes of a human being, not those of an academic futurist – as someone who is intensely fascinated by the human condition and raising human potential through the good times and the bad, at home and at work.

I throw my understanding of grief and loss into the mix too, because with any kind of change – by default or design – there is a need to let go of what was and accept what is. It is only through acceptance of the many paradoxes and ambiguities of life that we can truly live in the present, and not remain stuck in our past or frozen in fear about a future we cannot see. Self-leadership is the key.

This book is divided into five key sections, and it is essential that you read the first one, Dancing with Disruption, in its entirety for context. Thereafter, feel free to dip in as you wish.

Each chapter within each section also stands alone – as bite-sized opportunities for reflecting on different aspects of your life right now, with takeaways for winning at work, at home and in life. This means you can pick up this book at any time in your busy and demanding life for a dose of inspiration, guidance and hope, to help you in your many overlapping roles that are, in reality, all an expression of one person: you!

Just as I had the gift of a guide to take me safely home through the mist that night near Hilton when I was lost and afraid, I am offering to be your guide on this part of your journey as you emerge from your mist or open your door. Join me as I share lessons, insights, experiences, common-sense wisdom and simple tools to help you future-proof yourself from the inside out. You are not travelling alone, and you are more wired for change than you think!

Change is normal. It is not the end of the world – just the end of the world as you knew it.

Nikki Bush
Johannesburg
January 2021

FOREWORD

Nikki Bush has spent decades teaching and inspiring audiences and readers with her insights and exceptional wisdom. In a sterling career as a human potential and parenting expert, she has empowered people and companies to cultivate their strengths and rise to the demands of the twenty-first century. In a turbulent world, this is no mean feat. Her latest instalment, *Future-proof Yourself: How to Win at Work and Life*, could not have come at a more opportune time.

The world has been turned upside down by the unforeseen Covid-19 pandemic. Every single area of our lives has been irrevocably affected. All of humanity has been touched and disrupted, and Nikki immediately understood this impact. Her ability to go deep into the subconscious mind and expertly extract thoughts and words is impressive. With empathy and adeptness, she helps readers on their journey to find profound meaning and make sense of their state of mind.

Whether you are running an established business, or are an entrepreneur, employee, teacher, parent or child, learning how to respond to life's disruptions can mean the difference between life and death, success and failure. Nikki delivers these lessons in a warm, nurturing and empowering way.

But what makes Nikki so well positioned to frame complex emotions and experiences in ways that are accessible and inclusive? What is it about her world view and tone that makes the reader want to take the risk and begin a journey of self-discovery and learning?

Nikki doesn't just teach and share theories of life. In this book, with an amazing poignancy and vulnerability, Nikki boldly opens the door for us, allowing us to witness the darkest moment of her life, the most tumultuous disruption imaginable. Nothing in life could have prepared her for the devastating murder of her husband, Simon, and the split-second journey to widowhood and single parenting. In *Future-proof Yourself: How to Win at Work and Life*, Nikki truly dances with disruption and walks the path of loss, grief and trauma. In an act of generosity, she fills these pages with her vulnerability, bewilderment and courage. By sharing her story, Nikki leaves us in no doubt that the human spirit can triumph over adversity and navigate the unknown with courage, determination and a deeper understanding of the human condition. Covid-19 has been a time of grief, unemployment, financial distress, loss of autonomy and, for many, loss of loved ones. There can never be a better time to grab a copy and begin the path towards healing, self-discovery and growth.

Nikki has been a resident parenting expert on my award-winning radio show, *The Redi Tlhabi Show*, on Talk Radio 702 and 567 Cape Talk. She is a sought-after speaker and a trusted voice who has empowered families, educators and businesses to excel at life and build sustainable relationships. Listeners hang on to her every word as she delivers life's lessons with charisma and expertise. In this book she shares enduring lessons that will hold us in good stead as we learn to cope with the curveballs life throws at us.

Redi Tlhabi
Award-winning international journalist, author and moderator

SELF-REFLECTION

Exercise 1: Let's test your emotional temperature right now

How are you feeling *right now*? This is a question we sometimes avoid asking ourselves or others because we are afraid of what the answer might be. When you are working through any kind of disruption, change or loss in your life, it's good to take your emotional temperature from time to time. Stop trying to look good and get honest with yourself.

This is an exercise I do with every audience when discussing disruption, the current one being Covid-19. These days this takes the form of running an anonymous audience poll on whichever virtual-conferencing platform I am presenting on – whether my audience consists of twenty people or six thousand. The question helps to anchor delegates while giving me a benchmark for the group so that I can adapt my presentation as I go. So wear your honesty hat and allow yourself to become vulnerable and truthful as you answer these.

1. Name the disruption you are facing.

   ____

   ____

2. Circle which statement most accurately reflects how you are feeling *right now*, regardless of what disruption you are dealing with.

- Fearful and depressed
- Anxious and overwhelmed
- Reasonably in control
- Coping and confident
- Positive and optimistic about the future

There is nothing more you need to do with your answer just yet. Don't judge it. We will return to this exercise at the end of the book.

Exercise 2: Where is your thinking?

This is an interesting and unusual question that I share with permission from Caspar Craven, a friend and speaking colleague, from his book *Be More Human*: How much of your thinking is in the past, present or future? Honestly divide 100 per cent across these three categories and note down your scores.

PAST		PRESENT		FUTURE	

Now ask your spouse, friend or colleague (or your whole team at work) to do the same. You will be amazed at how different the results will be. The answers help us understand where each person is coming from. It can also be a gauge for how trapped you may be in your past, which could be limiting you in your present and in your future. Are you wishing for things to go back to the way they were? Do you own your past or does your past own you?

PART 1

DANCING WITH DISRUPTION

When things change dramatically, they rarely, if ever, go back to 'normal'. The way things used to be and the way things are will never be identical. The way you were and who you are now are different too. Disruption demands that we let go of the past and step into a new way of being. It's like a chemical reaction: nothing is ever the same again.

Think of the tides and the wind: we don't control them, but we can learn how to harness their power to work for us. When the wind comes up at the beach, on a dam or lagoon, the fair-weather bathers disappear and the adrenalin-junkie kite surfers and paragliders arrive, game to take on the wind and the tide. Just like them, we can learn new skills to deal with change. With patience, determination and practise we can improve our competence. We can build our confidence and gain a sense of control, even when everything feels out of control.

This is an image I shared with a young man who was very unhappy with how his life was turning out and was feeling victimised by circumstances. He found it empowering to think about disruption through this lens, identifying the tides and the winds in his life, and I helped him to come up with a plan to harness their power instead of being flattened by them. As Louisa May Alcott wrote, 'I am not afraid of storms, for I am learning how to sail my ship.'

How we frame the storms in our lives is very important. The storm image alludes to learning and growth versus giving up and feeling punished. More often than not, we discover more about ourselves and learn the most valuable lessons in our lives at the feet of pain, disappointment, frustration and disruption. If we see these storms as journeys of self-discovery about who we are and how we operate in the world, we can reframe these moments 'on our way, not in our way' – as human behaviour specialist Dr John Demartini puts it – to becoming bigger than, or more than, we were before the storm.

Dealing with disruption means actively *changing* or, more poetically, *dancing with change*, even when you can't actually see or touch the future. The doing is part attitude and part skills and action. Complaining and blaming will get you nowhere. Reading clever books, gleaning insights from thought leaders, connecting the dots and having 'aha' experiences mean nothing if you don't get off the couch, or out of your head, and actually *do* something. Without conscious action you will remain trapped in a prison of your own creation, limiting your ability to really embrace change and take advantage of all the possibility, learning and growth that come with it.

Coping with disruption demands flexibility, adaptability and resilience. Resisting change is fruitless and leads to distress, fear and frustration. I have learnt over time, and through my personal storms, that we have to move with it, much like in Aikido: when the attacking blow comes, you have to roll with it and move in the direction of the attack and the energy to minimise damage and buy yourself time to respond in the best possible way. There is a big difference between reacting in the short term and responding for long-term survival and growth.

Sometimes we are sent life tremors – warnings – and occasionally we are sent life quakes that shake us to the core and knock us off-centre. Whether you are responding to the global pandemic, getting married or divorced, becoming a parent, dealing with a significant death in your life, fighting a dread disease, or having to work remotely and in isolation for the first time, you must gather up your courage and walk into the storm. This requires:

- Visiting some dark places and uncomfortable emotions
- Taking self-reflection seriously
- Getting in touch with your feelings
- Taking responsibility for your role in whatever has happened
- Giving up naming, blaming and shaming
- Accepting the paradoxes and ambiguities that come with being human
- Managing your attitude and mindset by reframing and keeping perspective
- Taking action – even baby steps will do, but keep moving forward.

Talk is easy. Thoughts are plentiful. Action means:
- Taking a risk
- Stepping through the door into the unknown – the field of all possibility
- Trusting yourself – that you can handle this and figure things out
- Choosing not to be a victim of circumstance.

Are you going to resist disruption, or dance with it?

Chapter 1

Disruption is a catalyst for change

Disruption is never comfortable, but regardless of whether it is positive or negative, it is a catalyst for change. Change happens by chance, by choice, by crisis or calamity. The way we do things, live our lives, think and act is disrupted, and we have to find a new way of moving forward.

The dictionary definitions of disruption are 'a disturbance or problems which interrupt an event, activity, or process' and 'radical change to an existing industry or market due to technological innovation'.

This describes the disruption caused by the global pandemic, which will be with us for a long time as we transition and adjust to it. The same applies to a devastating divorce or the loss of a business. In any disruptive scenario that changes the way things are, you have to engage deeply with a process of adjustment and, ultimately, transformation.

It is easy to fall into the role of feeling like a victim when life throws you an unexpected curveball. Think about:

- death
- divorce
- accidents
- unplanned pregnancy
- loss of a business
- loss of health
- loss of wealth
- loss of a job
- loss of a home.

These are examples of unanticipated disruption. They change our carefully planned reality, breaking our picture of how life has been or what we think and believe life should be like. The degree and depth of disruption is often felt for a long time.

Even positive changes that we make by choice can leave us feeling uncomfortable for a time as we adjust. Think about:

- moving house
- moving town
- moving country
- starting a new job
- going to a new school
- striking out as an entrepreneur
- becoming involved in a new relationship
- getting married
- getting divorced
- becoming a parent.

Covid-19 is a perfect example of disruption and change that can be seen either as punishment or as a catalyst for change. Working with disruption to learn and grow from it is very different to kicking against disruption and getting stuck in a deep, dark hole devoid of possibilities and opportunities. The global pandemic has affected us in many different ways, changing how we run our lives and how we feel, right down to the most minute details, such as:

- where we work
- whether we can work
- whether our kids go to school
- whether we can worship
- how we bid farewell to loved ones we have lost
- how we physically touch and interact with each other as colleagues, friends and family
- freedom of movement/travel
- wearing masks
- overwhelming underlying fear (real or unfounded)
- a media onslaught of enormous negativity
- interruption of access to normal services for periods of time.

Disruption and change can be overwhelming. We would not be human if we didn't feel a variety of different emotions as we face losing control of our carefully constructed reality over which we feel in control. When we feel we are no longer holding the reins or can't see what lies ahead of us through the mist, there is a sense of chaos and insecurity around us and within us. We don't like it. Go ahead and circle the emotions you may have felt as you started dealing with the impact of the global pandemic on your life so far:

- unsettled
- fearful
- anxious
- out of control
- depressed
- overwhelmed
- shocked
- isolated
- invisible
- vulnerable
- unable to focus
- threatened
- incompetent
- insecure
- lacking confidence.

While these feelings all sound negative, pushing us completely out of our comfort zone and throwing us off course, they are actually perfectly normal. If you are like many of the delegates in my audiences, you may be breathing a sigh of relief hearing that these fears are normal and that it is appropriate to feel fear at this time.

Susan David, author of *Emotional Agility*, says it's good to embrace so-called negative feelings. In her 2017 TEDWomen talk called 'The Gift and Power of Emotional Courage' (a must-watch presentation), she explains how she conducted a survey with over 70 000 people and found that a third of us either judge ourselves for having what we believe are 'bad emotions', like sadness, anger or even grief, or actively try to push aside these feelings: 'We do this not only to ourselves, but also to people we love, like our children – we may inadvertently shame them out of emotions seen as negative, jump to a solution, and fail to help them to see these emotions as inherently valuable.'[1]

She calls this the tyranny of relentless positivity. 'Normal, natural emotions are now seen as good or bad. And being positive has become a new form of moral correctness. People with cancer are automatically told to just stay positive. Women, to stop being so angry. And the list goes on. It's a tyranny. It's a tyranny of positivity. And it's cruel. Unkind. And ineffective. And we do it to ourselves, and we do it to others .... But when we push aside normal emotions to embrace false positivity, we lose our capacity to develop skills to deal with the world as it is, not as we wish it to be.'[2]

DISRUPTION IS AN OPPORTUNITY TO RESET

We didn't ask for the coronavirus disruption; we didn't wish for it; we didn't invite it in – but we got it. It threw us all a curveball that we hadn't planned for and it has had a ripple effect on every aspect of our lives. It is making us reflect on and re-evaluate what is important to us today, and has us rethinking the future of our personal and professional lives. The question lingering in our collective minds is: What do we need to put in place to future-proof ourselves as best we can in the face of constant change? Is that even possible?

Of course, no one can be fully future-proof, but there are things you can do to prepare and manage yourself better to withstand the winds of change. Whether we like it or not, change is unavoidable in our personal lives, as are external disruptions due to the convergence of multiple technologies that have all been accelerated by Covid-19. If you think you are experiencing a speed wobble, you probably are, and that's because you *feel* you may be losing control. (Hint: control is a myth.)

Change brings with it fear of the unknown and fear of risk, but also the excitement of new adventures and possibilities – yes, you read that right! – no matter how awful you may be feeling right now. There will be mixed emotions as you let go of life or the world as it was, to embrace life as it is and will become in future. Put another way, you have to work with the world as it is, not as you wish it could be. This requires thinking differently – out of the box, constant learning, unlearning and relearning, problem-solving and extraordinary communication in a multitude of different ways.

When we have to face change, we may feel disempowered, but we don't have to give away our power. In fact, quite the opposite. Here's how you can remain empowered:

- keep perspective
- commit to self-reflection
- take responsibility for your choices
- take responsibility for your role in the situation
- embrace change; don't fight it, ignore it or resent it
- see the collateral beauty in the collateral damage.

If there is something the coronavirus has made us all sharply aware of, it's that control of our external world is largely an illusion. This is the very same lesson I learnt at 3.06 a.m. on 18 November 2017, when my family was attacked in our home in Johannesburg by armed intruders. Simon was murdered, taking a single shot to the heart. I had lost my husband. My sons had lost their father. In six short minutes our lives had changed forever.

Just as I cannot un-widow myself, neither can we un-Covid ourselves, as much as we may want to. There is only one way to go if we want to progress and grow, and that is forward!

Neither the loss of my husband nor Covid-19 are merely events, nor are they simply moments in time. They are very different examples of a process of adjusting to something traumatic that has happened without our permission. They are the epitome of disruption, calling us to reflect on and reset how we are going to move forward and 'be' in the world. How can we best future-proof ourselves emotionally to win at work and life in a century that futurists predict will be characterised by a magnitude of disruption we have never seen before? The coronavirus is just a taste of what's to come. As Manfred F.R. Kets de Vries, distinguished clinical professor of leadership development and organisational change at INSEAD, writes:

> Our response to this pandemic will have an enormous effect on the future of humankind. More than anything, the coronavirus has highlighted existing political, economic and social dysfunctionalities. It has also shown the crisis of leadership. It is an invitation to make radical changes to the economy, our social behaviour and the role of government in our lives.[3]

Takeaways for winning at work

- Keep perspective – don't panic if you don't have to
- Identify what you have control over: focus on that, and let the rest go – it will conserve your energy and keep you focused
- Honestly ask yourself whether things were perfect before the current disruption
    - What would you have changed then?
    - Does the current disruption move you any closer to making or achieving any of these changes?
- Disruption will bring with it a whole raft of different feelings
    - Find someone neutral with whom to work through your feelings, hopes and fears
    - Play 'worst-case scenario' and measure where you are against that; ask: 'What is the worst possible thing that can happen because of this?'
    - Work out your various options
    - The more you can process your feelings instead of locking them up, the less reactive you will be and the better you will handle things
    - You will clarify what you want or need and clearly ask for it
- If you are leading a team through the mists of disruption, what they want most from you is calmness and clarity
    - They need to see that you are human too, so it is good to be honest about your own feelings of unease and to identify with others – share your humanity
    - They need to feel confident in you
- Come up with a plan of action, even if it is only an interim plan until things become clearer
    - You need to learn how to lead from different places – from the front, from the back and side by side, depending on what is happening
    - Don't be afraid to ask your team how they are doing – and really mean it
    - Really listen to people – they are telling you what is important

    to them and they need to know that you have heard and understood them

- What your team members really need to know is that
    - You see them
    - You hear them
    - They are important to you
- What happens at home always has an impact on what goes on at work
    - Communicate enough about what you are going through to get the understanding and support you need as a member or leader of the team

Takeaways for winning at home and life

- By the very fact that we are human, we are changing all the time
- We are always in the process of becoming who we are
- Our evolution is constant: think about our physical, emotional and mental development as we age – from babyhood to childhood and from being a teen to becoming an adult
- Consider how we and our children move from
    - preschool to primary school to high school
    - to tertiary studies
    - and into the world of work
    - from retirement on to 'refirement' (creating a meaningful, productive and stimulating second half of our lives)
- Because we generally live longer, multistage lives, we must continue to find things to do to occupy us or make us money to live on
- Think about how we move into relationships, get married (and possibly divorced)
- Think about life experiences: injury, disease, trauma, death
- Take advantage of the pause that disruption brings with it – it is an opportunity to re-evaluate
    - what is important to us
    - who we are
    - whether we want to take advantage of a different direction at this time

- What happens at work always has an effect on what happens at home
  - communicate enough about what is happening at work for your family to understand why you might be quiet, irritated, stressed or upset
  - tell them how they can best support you
  - you might share part of your plan of action, if appropriate, so that they know that you have a plan

Chapter 2

Disruption on the horizon

The coronavirus pandemic is the opening act to a host of disruptions to come. In many ways it is accelerating all the disruptions that were already in progress before the pandemic. A disruption starts as a tremor that we barely notice – but it grows, like a rolling snowball, eventually having a knock-on effect on social structures, ethics, regulatory frameworks and much more. A case in point is that of social media giant Facebook being sued for failing to protect users' personal data in the Cambridge Analytica breach, which involved the use of harvested Facebook data of eighty-seven million people for, among other things, political advertising during the 2016 US elections. Another is ROSS, an artificial intelligence system that does legal research using IBM's Watson supercomputer. When an intelligent assistant can read forty million pages in fifteen seconds, it could ultimately replace entry-level attorneys doing discovery work for a case, showing how jobs will likely be lost and need to be recreated and reinvented.

I have been speaking about the topic of future-proofing and change since the publication of the first edition of *Future-proof Your Child* at the beginning of the global economic meltdown in October 2008, which I co-wrote with well-known expert on the future of work Graeme Codrington. The book is all about how to prepare our children for a fast-changing world. While it wasn't a prophecy, it contained a well-researched set of possibilities that all seem to have become reality a decade later.

In 2019, Graeme and I decided to write an updated tenth-anniversary edition called *Future-proof Your Child for the 2020s and Beyond* that sketched the magnitude and speed of the change to come. In it we said:

> As we look ahead to the 2020s and 30s, one theme stands out above all others: disruption. By this we mean that the way the world has worked up

> until now is going to change – and not just incrementally or predictably. The change is going to be deep and structural and result in new ways of doing things – the "rules of the game" are being rewritten, whatever "the game" happens to be. We are no longer absorbing change incrementally, but at a magnitude that is shaking up entire industries, destroying some in the process, and reshaping the way we do things both big and small.

Little did we know that a mere six months after publication the entire world would be plunged into a disruptive crisis – a global pandemic that would have an impact on every individual, family, town, country, continent, business and industry at the same time.

DISRUPTIVE CONCEPTS

People are waking up to the inescapable realities of disruption and realising that they are going to have to build the muscle to deal with it continuously as megatrends and converging technologies cause major shifts in all aspects of their lives. Every business or education conference anyone has attended in the past ten years has showcased some of them, all of which bring us ever closer to a connected world and an automated digital age. Here are just a few concepts you may or may not yet be aware of:

The Internet of Things

Everyday objects and systems will be connected to the internet via embedded sensors exchanging information, from smart cities to home security systems, to intelligent fridges and apps that tell you when to water your plants. Amazon Go stores allow you to simply pick your items off the shelf, they talk to your smart phone and you walk out – no teller required to complete the transaction.

Improved data storage and communication

There is enough digital storage capacity for all the information ever created in the history of the world. University College London has recorded the fastest data transmission speed of 178 terabits per second. At that rate, the entire Library of Congress – the world's largest library – could be downloaded in around one second. Apple's new M1 chip has sixteen billion transistors and is roughly the size of your fingernail. We can literally carry around super-computers in our pockets.

Data analytics

We are able to make sense of massive data sets, extracting useful information from them using smart data analytics algorithms to make decisions and predictions. When Boeing analyses take-off and landing information for its aircraft, the sensors generate as much information in ten take-offs as is stored in the Library of Congress. No human being could possibly go through all that information to extract the best parameters for take-offs and landings. Amazon will mine information on millions of books to match your reading preferences by using smart algorithms to analyse massive databases.

Artificial Intelligence and machine learning

Systems can learn from data, recognise patterns and make decisions with minimal human intervention, replacing repetitive jobs such as bookkeeping, basic research, computer programming, tracking our health and so much more. Auditing software Avenir is posing a challenge to the traditional role of accountants. Personal recommendations from the Netflix algorithm and targeted advertising on social media are perfect examples of machine learning and AI in action as are our smartphones – AI or IA (intelligent assistance) in our own back pockets – we go nowhere without them!

Quantum computing

Quantum computing has the potential to decode complex encryption a million times faster than normal computers. In the not-too-distant future, your encrypted WhatsApp messages may not be safe from prying eyes. (Stick with the rule of thumb to never share anything in an instant messaging app or on social media that you wouldn't want your mother to see!) Possibilities for advances in medicine and artificial intelligence are endless.

Transportation

The era of driverless vehicles is here. Linked to the Internet of Things – the network of physical devices connected to the internet – they will not only get you where you need to be, but will collaborate with other vehicles to determine the traffic pattern of the day and reduce road fatalities using sensors to analyse huge amounts of information in real time every second.

Robotics

Robotics are already widely used for repetitive tasks in manufacturing, and they have the potential to create more human unemployment as robots become smarter. Amazon has over 200 000 robots working inside its warehouse network alongside over a million human workers.

Virtual and augmented reality

Virtual reality immerses the user fully in an artificial digital environment via a headset. Augmented reality overlays virtual objects onto the real-world environment. Applications include interior design, driver training and virtual surgery, among many others.

A revolution in clean, cheap, renewable energy

As we move away from fossil fuels towards sustainable energy, we are developing wind, solar, hydro, geothermal, tidal, bioenergy and safe nuclear power. General Motors recently announced that the company will be phasing out petrol and diesel internal combustion engines and by 2035 will only be making clean-energy electric vehicles.

Energy storage

Energy storage and distribution is being developed that reduces both cost and impact on the planet: clean local energy generation per local community. There is a race to create advanced battery technologies for energy storage. A company in Estonia is developing a battery that can be charged in fifteen seconds. This will revolutionise the use of electric cars, cellphones and other devices.

Biotechnology

Biotechnology involves borrowing attributes from nature to enhance human life: growing meat from stem cells, creating external coverings for buildings that breathe like beetles do, and controlling heat exchange to reduce the use of air conditioning, for example.

Genetic engineering

In genetic engineering, scientists use recombinant DNA technology to alter the genetic make-up of an organism. Supercrops and the removal of faulty inherited genes are examples. This will bring with it ethical dilemmas as we tinker with human genes.

Geoengineering

Geoengineering is all about managing climate change and solar radiation, and carbon dioxide removal. Examples include spraying seawater thousands of metres into the air to seed stratocumulus clouds that will deflect sunlight, installing sun shields or mirrors in space to reflect the sun, and injecting sun-dimming particles into the atmosphere.

Materials engineering

This involves the creation of smart materials such as graphene. Two-hundred times stronger than steel, it is believed to be the strongest material yet discovered. It is both stiff and elastic like rubber, so it can be stretched up to 25 per cent of its original length without breaking.

New production methods

New production methods will fuel a global maker movement, allowing small businesses and individuals to collaborate to disrupt traditional large manufacturers and research and development (R&D) departments. This list contains a mere handful of converging technologies that are having an impact on every field, industry and area of study, facilitating remarkable breakthroughs and new ways of doing things. These technologies are driven by our ability to use machines to help us learn and apply our knowledge; they won't only affect the world of work, but will change society as a whole: how we do things, how we make decisions, how we communicate and how we build community.

We need to watch various trends that have the potential to affect us in many different ways, such as:

- Climate change: carbon emissions are contributing to rising temperatures; polar ice caps and glaciers are melting
- Refugees are moving country because of climate change, or because of religious or political persecution

- Populations throughout the world are ageing, except in developing countries
- The rich–poor divide is exacerbated by disruptive forces, such as a global pandemic
- Global politics is shifting trade, moving stock exchange indices, and polarising communities and countries
- Polarisation and division – just look at the impact of Donald Trump's presidency on America or the Covid-19 pandemic
- Global pandemics – Covid-19 will not be the last
- Biological warfare – the intentional release of viruses, bacteria and germs in acts of bioterrorism
- Stem cell research to treat Alzheimer's, leukaemia, spinal-cord injuries and more
- Biotechnology, such as new drugs, vaccines, and even enzymes that can keep food fresher for longer
- Space travel: the Mars One Project and Elon Musk's SpaceX are privatising space travel and exploration
- Renewable energy sources to save the planet and reduce carbon emissions
- Sustainable farming to avoid deforestation and grow produce closer to those it needs to feed
- Food security is a big issue and will increasingly become so as our planet's population heads towards twelve billion
- Water resources are dwindling; wars will be fought over fresh water instead of oil.

I will not unpack these issues in any further detail in this book; my focus here is on human behaviour and personal development aspects. This is why I highlight the findings of the World Economic Forum's *The Future of Jobs Report* of October 2020 on page 27 in this chapter. More about the trends reshaping the world of work can be found in *Future-proof Your Child for the 2020s and Beyond*, and in other titles in the recommended reading list at the back of this book, including Yuval Noah Harari's *Homo Deus* and *21 Lessons for the 21st Century.*

These and other disruptive forces will affect all aspects of your work and private world in unimaginable ways over the remainder of this century. If you need proof that change is afoot: research shows that 52 per cent of Fortune 500 companies have either gone bankrupt, been acquired or ceased to exist as a result of digital disruption.[4]

If you are reading this book, it is because you likely have a job or are self-employed and are part of the small percentage of the world's working population who can productively work from home owing to the nature of your work or your good fortune to have connectivity that enables you to do remote work. But let's pick up again on the disruption of the moment – the coronavirus. As we emerge from the mists, a number of things are becoming clear on the work front that are already affecting us, or will increasingly do so:

- Head offices and companies are fast realising that they don't need to have all employees in the office full-time
- Corporate jobs and the financial security that comes with a stable full-time salary with benefits will change as companies employ fewer people full-time and subcontract work out on a project basis
- Micromanagement within companies is becoming less possible in the work-from-anywhere culture, requiring individuals to manage themselves
- Periods of voluntary retirement to upskill and reskill may become the norm (for example, sabbaticals – often unpaid)
- Periods of unemployment will also become more common, which emphasises the importance of having multiple skills and different streams of income
- Self-leadership, being self-motivated and taking responsibility for your commitments will become the norm – people who can deliver will be hired and will be paid
- Raising energy, engagement and productivity will become the domain and responsibility of the individual
- Individuals will be responsible for their own learning journey and career trajectory, not the human resources department or the boss
- Individuals should be building a strong Brand of One with a compelling and ever-expanding talent profile so that they are job-ready within or outside their organisations as change happens or new opportunities arise
- It's time for individuals to claim back their power to choose how they live and run their lives, creating their own meaningful experiences

- We will be living longer, multistage lives instead of adhering to the traditional three-stage scenario of education–work–retirement
- We will need to become more savvy with our money and investments, as these will have to last for longer and fund periods of unemployment, voluntary retirement and our continuous learning journey
- We need to take more personal responsibility for our individual impact on the planet
- Looking after our own energy, mental and emotional health is paramount in an era of deep disruption that could see a mental-health crisis brought on by anxiety, fear and so many different kinds of loss
- With the shift to school from home during the pandemic, combined with technological disruption that was already on its way in, education will undergo a complete overhaul, and some children may never go back to traditional schools: some will stay online and some will find hybrid solutions; all of these developments will have an impact on how we live and work.

The double disruption of automation and the Covid-19 recession

The World Economic Forum released its *The Future of Jobs Report* in October 2020.[5] The report clearly confirms a double disruption due to automation and the Covid-19 recession. I share some highlights from the executive summary here, as these clearly confirm my observations and provide interesting clues as to what to expect on the human resources front:

- Adoption of new technology is expected to continue unabatedly, and its pace may accelerate in some areas
- Automation, in tandem with the Covid-19 recession, is creating a double-disruption scenario for workers
    - 43 per cent of businesses surveyed indicated that they are set to reduce their workforce owing to technology integration, 41 per cent plan to expand their use of contractors for task-specialised work, and 34 per cent plan to expand their workforce due to technology integration

- Although the number of jobs destroyed will be surpassed by the number of 'jobs of tomorrow' created, in contrast to previous years job creation is slowing while job destruction continues
  - By 2025 it is estimated that eighty-five million jobs may be displaced by a shift in the division of labour between humans and machines, while ninety-seven million new roles may emerge that are more adapted to the new division of labour between humans, machines and algorithms
- Skills gaps continue to be high as in-demand skills across jobs change in the next five years
  - Employers will increasingly be looking for employees with skills in areas such as critical thinking, analysis, problem-solving and self-management (including active learning, resilience, stress tolerance and flexibility)
  - On average, companies estimate that around 40 per cent of workers will require reskilling of six months or less, and 94 per cent of business leaders report that they expect employees to pick up new skills on the job (a sharp increase from 65 per cent in 2018)
- The future of work has already arrived for a large majority of the online white-collar workforce
  - 84 per cent of employers are set to rapidly digitalise working processes; this will include a significant expansion of remote work, with the potential to move 44 per cent of their workforce to operate remotely
- In the absence of proactive efforts, inequality is likely to be exacerbated by the dual impact of technology and the pandemic recession
  - Lower-wage workers, women and young people entering the workforce will be most affected
- Online learning and training is on the rise, but it looks different for those in employment and those who are unemployed
  - A fourfold increase in the numbers of individuals seeking out opportunities for learning online through their own initiative is likely

  - A fivefold increase in employer provision of online learning opportunities to their workers can be expected
  - A ninefold enrolment increase for learners accessing online learning through government programmes is predicted
  - Those in employment are placing more emphasis on personal development courses, which have seen 88 per cent growth among the population
  - Those who are employed are placing greater emphasis on learning digital skills such as data analysis, computer science and information technology
- The window of opportunity to reskill and upskill workers has become shorter in the newly constrained labour market
  - For workers who are set to remain in their roles, the share of core skills that will change in the next five years is 40 per cent, and 50 per cent of all employees will need reskilling
- Despite the current economic downturn, a large majority of employers recognise the value of human capital investment
  - On average, employers expect to offer reskilling and upskilling to just over 70 per cent of their employees by 2025, although employee engagement in those courses is lagging, with only 42 per cent of employees taking up employer-supported reskilling and upskilling opportunities
- Companies need to invest in better metrics of human and social capital through adoption of environmental, social and governance metrics, matched with renewed measures of human-capital accounting
  - Companies hope to internally redeploy nearly 50 per cent of workers displaced by technological automation and augmentation, as opposed to increasing lay-offs and making use of automation-based labour savings as a core workforce strategy
- The public sector needs to provide stronger support for reskilling and upskilling for at-risk or displaced workers

- Currently, only 21 per cent of businesses report being able to make use of public funds to support their employees through reskilling and upskilling
- The public sector will need to create incentives for investments in the markets and jobs of tomorrow, provide stronger safety nets for displaced workers in the market of job transitions, and decisively tackle long-delayed improvements to education and training systems.

NEW OPPORTUNITIES

Future-proofing yourself is a priority. Take up every opportunity to upskill and reskill offered by your employer, including digital skills and personal development. Our professional and personal lives have never been quite so closely intertwined, and I'm sure that you are already fast working out the domino effect of some of these trends. Here are a few examples close to home that may be familiar to you:

Education

- Parents who have relied on au pairs to fetch and drive around their children and supervise homework are replacing them with tutors (preferably qualified teachers) who can supervise their children's remote or rotational schooling
- Parents are converting their garages into schoolrooms and work with a tutor or teacher to provide more separation and supervision so that everyone is able to focus better
- Some parents, having experienced school from home, have decided home-schooling is an option for them and are prepared to take on the curriculum and make changes to their lives to embrace what they may consider a better form of work–life integration for the whole family. But school is not only about academics, so the education conversation will continue as various scenarios play out
- School is about to be reinvented. It was ripe for disruption, but there is no going back now. I anticipate that many more school formats will be

available to choose from in the future. The education arena will be an interesting space to watch.

The death of the three-stage life

- We are likely to live longer, and ever closer to an average lifespan of a hundred years
- The traditional three-stage life of education, work and retirement is disappearing
- Our own parents are living longer and outliving their pensions, which has an impact on us.

All of these factors will affect our personal financial planning, retirement age, accommodation arrangements, healthcare, ethics, multiple careers, lifelong learning and more. An interesting read on this topic is *The 100-Year Life: Living and Working in an Age of Longevity* by Lynda Gratton and Andrew J. Scott.

Business agility

The rules of the game have changed. The three examples below illustrate that if you have good reason to break the rules, it can, and should, be done.

- A B&B that went out of business overnight in lockdown decided to rent its rooms out to companies whose top executives were battling to work from home with children around. They were fully booked for socially distanced remote working in no time
- Early on in lockdown, the Netcare hospital group put out a request on a Facebook group for people with 3-D printers to each print ten units of the plastic head attachment for the face shields Netcare staff urgently needed, sharing the design online. Within a day or two they received all the parts they needed; it would have taken an average company two-and-a-half months to create only the mould! The rules of the game are changing dramatically, and so are the opportunities and the players. However, performance pressure will increase too
- Award-winning speaker and bestselling business author Douglas Kruger, a colleague of mine, was asked to write a book in seven days just before lockdown started owing to his track record of being able to produce a new book every six months. As an author myself, having written books

of 365 pages in four to six weeks, I know that to write one in seven days is extraordinary. But he did it! Not only did he rise to the challenge by collaborating with many business owners around the world for ideas on how to virus-proof small businesses during this challenging time, but the publishing house turned the book around from beginning to end in one month – something that had not been done before (four to six months is the industry norm).

No one is immune to the impact of disruptive trends now or in the future. Start reading and becoming more aware of what is trending on the horizon, particularly how it will affect your work and your family.

The chaos of disruption affects everyone differently. Regardless of who you are, where you come from and how you started out in life, you will be able to take advantage of new possibilities and opportunities. Individuals can now step up to the plate by accessing more choices, as they experience fewer barriers to entry. This gives them unprecedented opportunities to carve out a life of meaning – more than at any other time in history. It's all about how we choose to embrace the changes and disruptions we face: how courageous we are, our flexibility, and whether or not we are open to opportunities. Where you start out and where you end up will be largely up to you and the choices you make along the way.

Takeaways for winning at work

- Run regular What If™ sessions to work through possible scenarios that may have an impact on your business or your division[6]
- Look at different time horizons: one, three and five years (the meaning of short-, medium- and long-term has certainly changed!)
- Keep up to date with trends:
  - Research: give different team members different topics to track, research and report back on
  - Attend conferences and workshops on trends and report back to the team

- Keep an open mind
- Raise members of your team up to be resilient to cope with change – it's coming, whether you, or they, like it or not
- Take advantage of any upskilling or reskilling offered by your employer – prepare yourself before you need to
- Advancing your digital skills and your personal development are equally important at this time

Takeaways for winning at home and life

- The world isn't ending, it's just changing
- Disruptions mentioned in this chapter will change:
  - How we do things
  - How we make decisions
  - How we communicate
  - How we build and maintain community
- Keep up to date with trends both for yourself and for the sake of your children's future
  - What subjects should they study?
  - What qualifications do they need?
- Keep an open mind:
  - Think about your child's education and whether or not traditional schooling will serve them best (take your child as an individual and the requirements of the future world of work into account)
  - Does your child need to get a degree after school or is there a different path that may be far more useful?
  - There is no one-size-fits-all solution – each child is different
- Focus on helping your children develop the X factors for success that employers or clients will be looking for over and above their qualifications (read more about this in Chapter 20)

Chapter 3

Understanding why you feel threatened

The extent and duration of a crisis is something that we have little control over at first. Your job is to bring the chaos that emerges from a crisis into your locus of control as fast as possible.

– Pavlo Phitidis

Disruption is unfamiliar and uncomfortable. When we feel out of control, we feel threatened. Let's look at a little neuroscience from David Rock of the NeuroLeadership Institute, who details his SCARF model in his book *Your Brain at Work*. My interpretation of the model in the context of this book is that it gives us a simple framework with which to understand why we feel loss and change so acutely. It enables us to relate loss and change to various scenarios in life and helps us contextualise both our own fears and those of our family at home, or our team at work.

The basis of Rock's model is that we are either moving towards a threat or towards a reward. This has an effect on our feelings about five specific human needs, represented by the acronym SCARF:

- Status
- Certainty
- Autonomy
- Relatedness
- Fairness

Covid-19 provides a tangible illustration of the SCARF concept and how it relates to each and every person, and I am convinced that much of what I have included here will resonate with you. You can apply the concept equally well to any other challenge or disruption you face on your life journey.

Table 1: SCARF and Covid-19

BASIC HUMAN NEED	REWARD	THREAT
Status What gives you status in society?	A job; a source of income; shelter; food; healthcare; investments, etc.	Loss of job, income, title, home, health, wealth, etc.
Certainty What is your level of certainty about the future in the immediate, medium and long term?	Income stability; freedom to trade; children can go to school; planning a holiday	Will I become ill? Will I have a job? Will my business survive? Will my industry continue to exist? Will I still need a car? Will I be refunded for my missed holiday?
Autonomy How much freedom of choice do you have?	Choosing how many people to socialise with; ability to move about freely at any time of day or night; purchasing and drinking what you want when you want; deciding whether to work from home or the office	Not being able to travel; not knowing when you can go back to work from the office; no parties or funerals; no face-to-face strategic-planning meetings or team-building events
Relatedness How do you relate to others?	Hugging and shaking hands without fear; socialising freely; holding face-to-face meetings; feedback from others	Locked down and unable to socialise; loneliness; not free to meet others; limits to numbers at work or at social gatherings; missing children's graduations and weddings; seeing friends and colleagues only virtually
Fairness What's unfair about what is happening/ the situation?	Participating in rites of passage, such as matric dances, graduations and weddings; going to school; organising playdates	Unequal access to healthcare; cost of Covid testing; boredom; cancellation of weddings and graduation ceremonies; losing deposits for events; no sporting fixtures; no playdates for children; losing out on special occasions and celebrations; loss of income

The Covid-19 threats are very real. We are mourning what we have lost through disruption: our status, our freedom to choose, our freedom to move about, our freedom to work, our freedom to physically connect with other people, and so much more. Many people's freedom to earn a living has either been taken away due to restrictions or been lost as a result of the magnitude of economic disruption. We are caught in the mists of not knowing.

This loss of power over our own lives creates a broken picture. The picture of life as we knew it has cracked and can never be repaired to its original state. The process of grief about this loss of power is unique to every individual and is not linear. Nobody sails smoothly through Elisabeth Kübler-Ross's well-known five stages of grief (which generally apply to all forms of loss, including death, divorce and break-ups, among others); instead, we flip-flop backwards and forwards between denial, bargaining, anger, depression and acceptance; we can be through a stage and then be thrown back into it again.

The key is to eventually reach acceptance and be able to embrace the paradoxes and ambiguities of life that accompany competing demands that cannot be eliminated or resolved. Work and family life continue regardless of what happens to us and our choices. An either/or approach will hold us prisoner to a black-and-white way of thinking. The world we live in is increasingly showing up in multiple shades of grey. As Arthur Goldstuck and I wrote in our book *Tech-savvy Parenting*, we now live in a both/and world. We have to get comfortable with craving certainty yet having no clarity, with being dependent on screens yet craving human connection, with being tough and yet loving.

Adopting a paradox mindset is essential for us to balance competing demands that have become even more apparent in the current global lock-down, say Ella Miron Spektor, associate professor of organisational behaviour at INSEAD, and Wendy Smith, professor of management and co-director of the Women's Leadership Initiative at the University of Delaware: 'We not only face tensions between work and family, but also between making decisions for the short-term and the long-term, or ensuring physical isolation while enabling social connection. An either/or approach can lead to limited solutions and personal suffering, whereas adopting a paradox mindset actually boosts innovation, creativity and performance. The way we interpret our reality is vital, especially in a time of crisis.'

They freely share their simple three-step framework to help adopt a paradox mindset.

THE PARADOX MINDSET – A THREE-STEP FRAMEWORK

Step 1: Reframe the question
We might, for example, change the question 'Should I pivot or continue with what I have been doing?' to 'How can I both continue and pivot? How can one help the other? How can the way I have always been doing things provide me with the assets and resources to help me change to something new? How could the energy and potential from adopting something sustain me as I continue to do the things I still need to get done?' By changing the question, we discover new ways to do both.

Step 2: Accept the tension and develop comfort with the discomfort
With the paradox mindset, acceptance allows for the understanding that these tensions are a natural part of reality, and that we all experience them to a certain extent. (See my Collateral Damage vs Collateral Beauty exercise on page 47 for a practical exercise you can do now.)

Step 3: Distance yourself and search for new possibilities
When you feel torn by competing demands, connect with others for a different perspective or pretend you are making decisions for someone else. We are more likely to come up with creative solutions in this way.

Paradoxical thinking happens when people see the tensions and paradoxes approaching and surrounding them as opportunities for creativity, learning and growth. They can see both the threats and the rewards in the SCARF model, embrace the both/and of paradoxical thinking, and can spot the reinvention gap these present. If you can embrace paradox and ambiguity, you will be better positioned, mentally, to future-proof yourself.

Takeaways for winning at work

- Have a discussion about threats with your team
- By identifying the threat and bringing it out into the open, you can diffuse some of its power
- You start the shift away from helplessness and hopelessness when you know what you want to move towards (the reward) and what you need to do to get there (the plan)
- You have a better perspective of what is at play instead of being overwhelmed by too many unnamed threats; this reduces paralysis and you are better able to harness productivity and engagement
- We live in a both/and world, so ditch the either/or mindset
- Use the three-step paradox mindset framework for discussions

Takeaways for winning at home and life

- Parental anxiety is more infectious than any disease on the planet
- You are like the weather: you set the emotional temperature in your home
- Your children will pick up cues from you
- Deal with your own stress and anxiety as best you can
- Be honest but age-appropriate in how you talk to your children about why they or you may be feeling threatened
- Ask them how they are feeling – don't guess
- Ask them what they know – again, don't guess
- Really listen, and reflect what they say back to them to make sure that they know you have understood
- If you are in a supportive relationship, share your fears with your partner instead of bottling them up
- If you cannot talk to your partner for whatever reason, or you do not have a significant other, find a neutral person to talk you through what's going on inside you
- Be careful of your self-talk when you experience competing demands: try to reframe them as both/and rather than either/or

Chapter 4

The journey to acceptance of disruption

While disruption can make us feel incredibly threatened, it invites us to step into a process of adjustment and transition. The word 'process' is important here; it means we move through various stages as we internalise change.

I interviewed veteran educator, counsellor, speaker and author Dereck Jackson about the seven stages of adjustment and transition that he has been teaching for many years. 'Knowing there are various stages that one moves through and circles back to gives you a starting point for the journey,' he told me. 'Knowledge is power and, strangely enough, knowing there is a pathway provides a modicum of comfort – knowing that others have walked this path before and survived. Make no mistake, even positive changes like marriage, becoming parents, changing jobs, or moving homes or countries require us to move through the same stages.' It is important to distinguish the difference between an event and a process. Dereck provides an example we can all relate to: a wedding is an event, while a marriage is a process that goes on for the duration of the relationship.[8]

In this chapter I unpack Dereck's seven stages model (refer to the diagram at the top of page 40), which I have found unbelievably helpful in both the Covid-19 crisis and while dealing with the trauma and adjustment that came with becoming a widow. The model is spot on and may be helpful to you too, whatever loss or change you may be experiencing right now or in the future, be it a job change, your children starting at a new school, or losing a loved one.

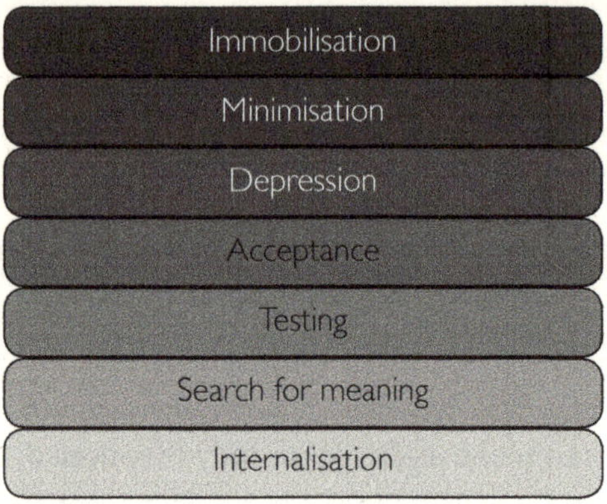

Figure 1: The seven stages of adjustment and transition model

IMMOBILISATION

- Initially we become immobilised by our fear; we are frozen
- We find reasons not to do something, even if it is a positive change that we really want – such as taking on a new job or a promotion at work, or a child moving to a new school
- We may develop psychosomatic symptoms: children who transition from primary to high school may develop a stomach ache, someone starting a new job may experience backaches, and the stresses of Covid-19 may spark headaches; we try any excuse to not get out of bed and step into the unknown
- We resist change even if we seek it.

MINIMISATION

- This stage calms us down because we find ways to minimise the threat. A sibling going to a new school thinks, 'If my brother could do this and he's so shy, then so can I!', or we might think, 'Only old people die from the coronavirus, so I'll be okay.' (In the early stages of lockdown I kept telling myself that if Victor Frankl and Nelson Mandela could survive incarceration, then I could survive lockdown; after all, their situation was far worse!)

DEPRESSION

- We feel low and down in the dumps
- We think negatively: 'I can't do it'; 'I don't have any friends'; 'I can't have my party in lockdown'; 'It's not fair!'; 'Who do I think I am that I can do this job?'
- This type of reaction is normal and represents withdrawal from our current reality where we *think* we would prefer not to be, even if we have chosen it – like a new job
- We might visit our previous employer for validation, or your child might ask to visit the school they recently left. There is a secret hope that they will tell us how much they miss us or will offer to take us back. You discover they are too busy to spend much time on you and they don't offer you your place or job back – this might be a shock, but it's also a reality check
- You don't believe you have the resources or skills for the challenge or task at hand, and you feel unconfident and incompetent. These beliefs contribute to us feeling down. This is why it is important to take intentional action to move away from threat and towards reward, in line with the SCARF model, if you want to shift out of depression
- When it comes to children, mothers sometimes create more problems than there are by wanting to take their child's pain away instead of helping the child work through the problem. It is wise to remember that when we allow someone to work through a problem or challenge we are helping them build resources and coping mechanisms for the present and the future. Allow others to own their own problems by discovering their own solutions.

ACCEPTANCE

- We now know we have to deal with the change or the problem
- We know we can't go back, and that we have to move forward
- Just as I cannot un-widow myself, none of us can un-Covid ourselves
- On the way to acceptance of change and our new reality we may revert to previous stages by sliding back into depression before moving forward into the testing phase.

TESTING

- We find ourselves accepting that we are in a new reality and we start to test it
- We try new ways of doing things in this new space until we find something that works; we are now on our way to rewiring our beliefs about ourselves, our actions and our behaviour
- A great example is when a child at a new school tries to make new friends: if the strategy works, they do it again; if it fails, they try another way
    - The problem with Covid-19 lockdown is:
    - Governments are in control of setting the pace of transition, causing frustration
    - We don't have the opportunity to fully test our new reality, which can lead to irritation
    - As lockdown eases we start accepting our new reality and we want to test it, but for now, or as lockdowns are implemented with further infection surges, we feel stuck
    - Parents who are now guiding their children through school from home are feeling inadequate, which can push them back into depression
    - The stop–start nature of lockdown makes us feel out of control and frustrated
    - Children who thought their parents knew everything and could solve any problem are now seeing their parents at the mercy of institutions and government; this can lead to disappointment and depression
    - Confidence can be affected or even shattered if testing our new choices, actions and behaviour is not optional, such as children not going back to school physically, international travel being on hold if you earn your living from tourism, not being able to have all your employees back in the office because of social-distancing requirements, and limits on exhibitions, conferences and the restaurant trade
    - We have to become unstuck before we can move forward and disengage from insisting that things go back to the way they were
    - During the testing phase, we start to compare our new reality with our old reality – our new life with our old life, our new normal with our old normal.

MEANING

- We are able to look back at where we were and find meaning
- We can make sense of our new situation and see the bigger picture
- Growth is within our grasp.

INTERNALISATION

We realise we have learnt new skills during this adjustment and transition period; for example:

- We have learnt to deal with boredom
- We have learnt to make friends with loneliness
- We have become more independent and resourceful
- We have embraced a new reality
- We are able to live with paradoxical thinking, shifting away from the limits of either/or to both/and thinking
- We get to a point where we can declare, 'I'm happy with my new life'
- We display flexibility and adaptability.

Everyone goes through the same seven stages of adjustment and transition. Some will do so faster. Some will need more time. Remember that there is no timeline. Don't get hooked on a date or a period of time. Step into the process, trusting that you will survive, and keep moving. Embrace each stage, no matter what it feels like. If you need support, get it. Don't get stuck in 'fight, flight or freeze' mode. If you declare, 'I can't cope – I'm stuck!', you are still wishing for what you can't have. You become a prisoner of your own making and a victim of circumstance. Find a way to get yourself unstuck.

All change and losses become part of the fabric of our lives – part of our history and narrative. The important thing is to ask ourselves: 'What have I learnt from this?' and 'How have I grown from it?' This is only possible when we get to the stages of acceptance, internalisation and finding meaning. I hope an understanding of the seven stages will help you as much it has helped me to reframe and rewrite my life story.

Takeaways for winning at work

- Remember that there is a difference between an event and a process – processes will take time and you need to be empathetic, but also firm and supportive of your team
- This process may open up the potential for members of your team to leave or stay, depending on what emerges for them during their process
- The seven stages of adjustment and transition apply to the loss of a colleague through a job shift, or even death, as well as to changes in businesses due to a buyout, downsizing, or the threat of temporary or permanent closure
- Create a safe space where team members can share where they are in the process; you will probably see that they are all in different places. This will affect their productivity and performance

Takeaways for winning at home and life

Some words of advice for the journey through the seven stages:

- Don't try to stop a stage; support yourself, your children or your friends through each stage
- If parents handle the transition well, their children will usually handle it well too
- Cry – please cry! – but also get better
- Don't try to push a child into a stage if you feel they should be depressed just because you are
- You should not rush an emotion or a stage either
- Create a positive belief system; believe that you can and will cope
- It's not what happens to you that is a problem, it's what you do about it
- Take responsibility for your own emotions, actions and behaviour
- Use the power of choice; choice is never fully taken away from you
- Instil a daily routine for predictability, structure and sanity
- If you need support, ask for help from a counsellor, coach or therapist; join support groups for help with depression, anxiety, suicidal thoughts, addiction, parenting support or divorce recovery;

search the internet; ask for referrals; tap into the employee-assistance programme at work (larger employers usually provide basic legal, financial, medical and psychological support if your company has registered their employees with one of these service providers)
- Bear in mind that loss, trauma, grief and any emotional pain are not experienced merely in your head and heart but can get trapped in your body too; body and energy work can be extremely helpful in integrating change and adjustment
- I have found these techniques an invaluable part of my toolkit at different times: Eye Movement Desensitisation and Reprocessing (EMDR), Body Stress Release, hypnotherapy, Emotional Freedom Technique (EFT), meditation, Tension and Trauma Release Exercises (TRE), Reiki, reflexology, Energy Vortex Balancing, craniosacral therapy, massage and various others
- If you are religious or a person of faith you may find solace and comfort in worship, praying, reading and studying the scriptures that support your faith

Chapter 5

Keeping perspective

If we are unable to keep perspective in disruptive times, we run the risk of getting stuck in negative emotions and end up feeling completely overwhelmed or buried by them. But if, instead, we are able to hold on to perspective and accept the ambiguities of life, we empower ourselves and can keep our fears in proportion.

It's easy to see only the damage, the negative aspects of disruption, and to miss the attendant collateral beauty. This is another paradox of disruption: that we need to hold both the damage and the beauty together, for therein lies learning and growth, and therein lies the balance, if we can see it. The paradox provides us with a gift of perspective.

During the first year following my husband's murder there were times when I got extremely angry – with him, with the world and with my country, which I felt had betrayed me and turned my life upside down. As a speaker I was being asked to share my story from a platform, and this brought me to a point of having to package a very messy, complicated, non-linear and shocking experience into a linear presentation filled with teachable moments to help others deal with disruption in the future. It required a lot of soul-searching and reflection and, to be honest, the initial preparation for this presentation as a widow of just nine months pushed me into a state of complete post-traumatic stress and shock as I relived the experience.

But part of processing trauma, loss and grief is working through the experience you have had, so this process of analysing and packaging my experience became its own form of therapy. Amid my anger and frustration, as I was working out what would be helpful to others, I found myself sitting in bed one Sunday morning contemplating the presentation, asking myself: 'Is there anything good coming out of what happened to us?' So I folded a piece of paper in half vertically down the middle and wrote 'collateral damage' at the top of the left-hand column and 'collateral beauty' on the right.

I started listing things on the collateral-damage side first. Using the technique of stream-of-consciousness writing, I wrote down whatever came to mind, with no judgement: a feeling or an emotion; a person; an experience; the fact that I had lost my husband and my children had lost their father; I had lost the future co-grandparent to my grandchildren; my husband would never be at our sons' weddings; we lost our home in the process – on and on I wrote. I vented on that page. Every last negative thing I could think of or feel in that moment I cleared out of my head and heart. You have no idea how much lighter I felt after writing down two-and-a-half pages of collateral damage I had suffered.

When I could write no more, I turned to the collateral beauty side of the page and got going in the same vein. Anything positive that had happened as a consequence of my husband's death – a person who had walked into my life and made a difference; good experiences; emotions (yes, even gratitude, opportunities and possibilities that had never been there before). I wrote and wrote and wrote, giving meaning to this line that I still cling to today: 'There is meaning hidden in the small changes of everyday life, and wisdom to be found in the shards of your most broken moments,' writes Elizabeth Lesser in her book *Broken Open: How Difficult Times Help Us Grow.*

The collateral-beauty list turned out to be five pages long – twice as long as my collateral-damage list. This realisation blew me away and changed my perspective about what had happened to me. It gave me a new lens through which to view my experience and provided me with a framework that I have found useful for many different disruptions, including moving house, dealing with Covid-19, entering into a new relationship, deciding whether to consider brand association with different companies, and so much more.

The Collateral-Damage vs Collateral-Beauty exercise is part of my Collateral Damage Repair Process©. It is also an exercise I share regularly with audiences in my talks or during media interviews. Those who do the exercise all report being astounded by their discovery of how much positive there is among the damage. It helps them embrace the paradox more comfortably and realise that new possibilities and opportunities are sitting right there on the right-hand side of the page.

Of course, I know some of the damage in a particular situation could be very serious and will have long-term consequences. We need to identify all the collateral damage we have experienced and acknowledge it. The feelings that go with it are very real and should not be suppressed. However, if you get stuck in a collateral-damage mindset, you will become frozen in fear, anger, frustration, irritation, despair and much more. There will be no room for growth and reinvention. So go there, but don't get stuck there!

To actively balance out the collateral-damage list, I urge you to look at the collateral-beauty list too. Write down anything and everything you can think of that is positive or potentially good about the disruption you are experiencing – whether it be a divorce, Covid-19, a job change, or something else entirely. This is where growth, opportunity and hope live. I promise.

MY COLLATERAL-DAMAGE VS COLLATERAL-BEAUTY EXERCISE FOR COVID-19

Just before doing a radio interview in the worst stages of hard lockdown, I spent ten minutes (yes, just ten minutes!) doing this exercise on the back of a piece of scrap paper while waiting to go on air to help people cope with the unfamiliar and challenging position in which they found themselves. This is what my two lists looked like, and I have continued adding to them. I shared this exercise with my listeners too.

Collateral damage

- Social distancing
- Social isolation
- Loneliness
- Fear
- Fatigue
- Unknown future
- Feeling out of control
- Loss of freedom to move about
- Loss of choice
- Dozens of presentations cancelled or postponed
- Cash-flow issues

Collateral beauty

- Appreciate people more
- Value relationships
- Gratitude (go into details if you wish: health, specific people, acts of kindness, etc.)
- Time at my disposal because I am not racing around
- Slowing down
- Reset opportunity
- Reinvention
- Innovation
- I'm ready for this!

- No big family gatherings
- Working from home with my boys in an open-plan rental
- Not having a dedicated room I can convert into an office-cum-TV studio
- Can't celebrate my sister's 50th birthday with her
- Potential illness
- 24/7 negative news reporting
- Fake news
- Poor role models in the current situation
- Panic buying
- Greed
- The disparity between rich and poor
- People who add to the negativity in your life

- Expression of human emotions
- Unity with others
- Honesty
- Kindness
- Getting real
- Stopping
- A reminder that we always have a choice
- Our power lies in each moment
- Adventure of the unknown
- Curiosity about the future
- Gaining self-knowledge
- Testing my resilience
- Proving my adaptability
- Flexible mindset
- Brush up on tech skills
- Learn new skills: lighting, cameras, webinars, etc.
- Using new tools
- Quality family time
- Self-development
- Time to tie up some loose ends for peace of mind
- Repositioning
- Excitement
- Challenge
- New ways to exercise
- Creative cooking with the ingredients I have
- Baking
- Reading
- Journaling
- Doing some online courses
- New mindfulness and meditation practices
- People who are adding to the positivity in my life
- Prioritising: What's really important?

These lists are obviously not complete or exhaustive – they were a first quick download from my head and my heart. I found it helpful to visualise them in the form of the two side-by-side columns. I believe this gives us perspective.

Part 2 delves into one of the disruptive trends that has turned our lives inside out and upside down and one that will continue into the foreseeable future: remote working and working from home.

Takeaways for winning at work

- I challenge you to do the Collateral Damage vs Collateral Beauty exercise for Covid-19 in your capacity as a leader or a team member
- Then, if you lead a team, and you are facing a common threat or challenge, do the process together
- Revisit it regularly during the crisis you are facing to add to both sides of the list
- See how the lists link to where you are within the seven stages of adjustment and transition model (see page 40)

Takeaways for winning at home and life

- I challenge you to do the Collateral Damage vs Collateral Beauty exercise for Covid-19 for yourself as soon as possible
- Then, if you are a couple, do it together
- Finally, if you are a family, do it as a group exercise
- Revisit and add to both lists on a weekly basis
- See how the lists link to where you are with the seven stages of adjustment and transition model (see page 40)

PART 2

WORKING REMOTELY

If you are someone who has been able to work from home during the pandemic, you are probably in a field such as finance, insurance, management, business services or information technology – careers most suited to remote working. The debate about flexible working has long been on the table, but the discussion turned into a mass global work-from-home experiment overnight due to the pandemic, and we are its live subjects.

Although we have had access to virtual-conferencing tools such as Zoom and Skype, and productivity tools such as Microsoft Teams and Slack for some years, they were mostly used by multinational businesses to help them work across time zones and geographical borders. Then Covid-19 came along. Overnight, office workers were sent home to work remotely, and tools such as these became the mainstays of business without which we couldn't operate.

Business continuation was possible due to technology. The heroes in businesses right now are often the facilitators who know these systems and have been able to onboard and get employees up to speed quickly – not an easy feat in large organisations with thousands of employees who needed the hardware, secure systems access and connectivity to be able to operate and do their jobs.

Beyond the systems, the way we think about work itself has been challenged, including the hours we work, where we work from, and whether commuting and appearing in person at the office is really necessary or will be necessary in the future. Out of necessity and urgency we had to act differently to keep the wheels of business and economies turning, and in the process we have experienced a mindset shift among both employers and employees across the board about what is possible.

While employment practices have largely been based on company processes and profit, we will see human resources policies and practices being revised, putting the human in the middle and becoming more family friendly. Gradually, employees will become less dependent on, and more independent of, input from management to do their job. Companies are discovering that they don't need to hold on to so much office space, if any, and they don't need to employ so many people full-time and will prefer to subcontract and buy services in as required.

With this will come a shift from total dependency on organisations to greater self-leadership. While there will be less job security, there will also be much more freedom of choice for people who might choose to join the on-demand gig economy by selling their services back to corporates via online platforms or starting up their own businesses. According to Global Workplace Analytics:[9]

- People are tired of the rat race, eager to take control of their lives, and desperate to find a balance between work and life
- 79 per cent of people want to work from home
- 36 per cent would choose it over a pay rise
- A poll of 1 500 technology professionals revealed that 37 per cent would take a pay cut of 10 per cent if they could work from home
- Millennials are more difficult to recruit (as reported by 56 per cent of hiring managers) and to retain (as reported by 64 per cent of hiring managers), but they are particularly attracted to flexible work arrangements (ranked eight on a ten-point scale for impact on overall job satisfaction)

- 80 per cent of employees consider work from home a job perk.

What started out as short-term restrictions, forcing a remote-work culture to develop, has morphed into long-term opportunities for individuals and businesses. Companies such as Dropbox, Shopify and Twitter have said they will embrace remote working after Covid, while many companies are starting to look at how they can create a hybrid and more flexible approach to work that maintains the efficiencies of remote working by incorporating the needs for human beings to connect face to face.

Some of the many benefits include:

- Increased employee retention
- Reduced absenteeism
- Increased productivity
- Increased collaboration
- Expansion of the talent pool
- Keeping retirees in the talent pool
- Scaling the workforce up and down easily
- Continuity of operations in case of disaster
- Increase in employee empowerment.

While there is, on some level, a deep sense of loss of what was, there is also curiosity about what might be possible and how we might co-create a new way of working that may be more workable and healthier for everyone. As much as we like to think things were perfect before the pandemic, they weren't. Companies were struggling with low employee engagement and productivity, and employees were battling with stress, elusive work–life balance and not finding meaning in their work.

Out of crisis and necessity, a mass global work-from-home experiment has begun, and we are all part of it.

Chapter 6

Working from home

Before the pandemic, the work-from-anywhere trend was starting to take hold in small pockets largely made up of entrepreneurs. They were people who, like me, worked from home and would have meetings in 'third spaces' (not the home, but also not in an office) – spaces where everyone is on purpose. They went there to work, but the spaces had a vibe: good coffee, good food, good connectivity, a boardroom, and sometimes hot-desking options and more. The dramatic shifts in this arena that took place overnight due to lockdown restrictions during the coronavirus pandemic meant that everyone who was able to work remotely had to do so, and they had to do so from home. The work-from-home economy was born, and it looks as though this trend is here to stay long after the pandemic dies down.

Whether businesses had twelve employees or six thousand, as some of my clients had, they were sent home to work with forty-eight hours' notice. The logistical disruption was immense, but companies rallied – as they tend to do in a crisis. Some were better prepared than others. According to DataFirst,[10] only 13.8 per cent (two million people) of the employed South African population can feasibly work from home. These are largely managers, professionals and employees in the tech and financial services sectors. They are people who can do their jobs on computers. Connectivity issues, lack of access to hardware and a small pool of skilled workers contribute to this low figure in South Africa.

According to Stanford economist Nicholas Bloom:

> In the US 42 per cent of the labour force is now working from home full-time. About another 33 per cent are not working – a testament to the

> savage impact of the lockdown recession. And the remaining 26 per cent – mostly essential workers – are working on their business premises. So, by sheer numbers, the US is a work-from-home economy. Almost twice as many employees are working from home as at work. More strikingly, if we consider the contribution to US gross domestic product based on their earnings, this enlarged group of work-from-home employees now accounts for more than two-thirds of US economic activity.[11]

But those who are able to do their work remotely don't necessarily have ideal working conditions in which to do so. This is a challenge companies are having to overcome. Roz Broome, chief operating officer of Capability BPO, a company that sets up and runs international customer service call centres for the likes of Groupon and Instacard from South Africa, says sending an employee home with the hardware to do their job is one thing. But then you discover they have no furniture – not even a desk. You also find out they are sharing a room with many people, have no privacy and their area suffers regular power outages, and you need to use a heat map to work out which service provider to use for data so that they have access to connectivity. It's a minefield that entails having to deconstruct and reinvent businesses with remote workforces, but it has to be done. Inequalities in society are showing up in technicolour – not only in South Africa, but all over the world.

The work-from-home shift was not only a logistical nightmare for businesses but required massive adjustment for the majority of employees who had never worked from home before. Effective working from home (sometimes abbreviated as WFH) is an acquired set of skills, and it takes time to sharpen one's saw. I can attest to this, having worked and built a business and brand from home as a solopreneur for the past twenty-five years.

According to McKinsey's *Future of Work Report: What's Next for Remote Work*,[12] an analysis of 2 000 tasks and 800 jobs in nine countries, the potential for remote work depends on the mix of activities undertaken in each occupation, and on their physical, spatial and interpersonal context.

FROM MCKINSEY'S *THE FUTURE OF WORK REPORT*

We first assessed the theoretical extent to which an activity can be done remotely. This depends on whether a worker needs to be physically present on-site to do a task, interact with others, or use location-specific machinery or equipment.

Many physical or manual tasks, as well as those that require use of fixed equipment, cannot be performed remotely. These include providing care, operating machinery, using lab equipment, and processing customer transactions in stores. In contrast, activities such as information gathering and processing, communicating with others, teaching and counselling, and coding data can theoretically be done remotely.

Additionally, during the pandemic employers have found that although some tasks can be done remotely in a crisis, they are much more effectively done in person. These activities include coaching, counselling, and providing advice and feedback; building customer and colleague relationships; bringing new employees into a company; negotiating and making critical decisions; teaching and training; and work that benefits from collaboration, such as innovation, problem-solving and creativity. If onboarding were to be done remotely, for instance, it would require significant rethinking of the activity to produce outcomes similar to those achieved in person.

For instance, while teaching has moved to remote work during the pandemic, parents and teachers alike say that quality has suffered. Similarly, courtrooms have functioned remotely but are unlikely to remain online going forward out of concern for legal rights and equity – some defendants lack adequate connectivity, and lawyers and judges worry about missing non-verbal cues in video conferences.

According to Statista,[13] these are the most significant struggles respondents have had while working remotely:

- Difficulties with collaboration – 20 per cent
- Loneliness – 20 per cent
- Not being able to unplug – 18 per cent
- Distractions at home – 12 per cent
- Being in a different time zone to teammates – 10 per cent
- Staying motivated – 7 per cent
- Taking vacation time – 5 per cent

- Finding reliable Wi-Fi – 3 per cent
- Other – 5 per cent.

Needless to say, working from home has been far easier for some than for others. Those with young children have had a much rougher ride in terms of adapting, especially as most homes do not have separate office spaces precisely because they didn't need them when the adults were working at the office. Sharing spaces with children will be discussed in detail in the next chapter.

It is predicted that those who can continue to work from home, or remotely, will continue to do so two to three days per week. We can expect hybrid working models to emerge, depending on our line of work, which will challenge the rigidity of how we, as individuals and organisations, view time. For example, do we need the five-day work week and a nine-to-five workday? Ricardo Semler raised this issue in his bestselling book *The Seven Day Weekend*, as did Tim Ferriss in *The 4-Hour Work Week*.

Indications that Covid-19 will permanently transform modern working life is already evident in large organisations such as Unilever, one of the UK's largest companies, which have said that their office workers will never return to their desks five days a week.[14] J.P. Morgan, one of the world's largest investment banks, is making plans for its more than 60 000 workers to continue with remote working.[15]

A Gartner survey of company leaders found that 80 per cent plan to allow employees to work remotely at least part of the time after the pandemic, and 47 per cent will allow employees to work from home full-time. In a PricewaterhouseCoopers survey of 669 CEOs, 78 per cent agreed that remote collaboration is here to stay for the long term.[16]

Microsoft Japan's experiment with a four-day work week in 2020 resulted in a 40 per cent rise in worker productivity – in an era in which management and human resources have been battling with only 10–15 per cent of employees being engaged and productive at work. This proves the point that we allow our work to fill the time available. Watch this space.[17]

Takeaways for winning at work

From the work I have done with dozens of large employers who have empty corporate campuses and thousands of employees working from home, as well as some smaller SMMEs, I have distilled twelve months of feedback, gathered from this live experiment, which should be taken into consideration to enhance the work-from-home experience. The list is not exhaustive, but includes the most common feedback:

- Have fewer conference calls or group meetings
    - Only hold conference calls *with everyone* if it is necessary
    - There are a multitude of ways to communicate without having to disrupt everyone's workflow
    - Use asynchronous communication channels more efficiently, including texts, emails, group messages via the company productivity platform, sending a video or audio recording to get the same message across to everyone quickly without wasting their time
- Have social catch-ups separately to business meetings
    - Meetings become too long and drawn out when trying to do both
    - We overcompensate for lack of human interaction by spending half an hour catching up around the room before we get to the business end; this is exhausting
- Create a no-meeting time zone
    - Some of my clients have decided on no meetings between 12 p.m. and 2 p.m. every day or during the first hour of work in the morning
    - What employees do in this time is up to them – whether it is catching up on focused work, eating lunch with their families or getting chores done
    - Some companies have meetings-free days
- Set non-video calls by default
    - I never thought I would be saying this, but once you have seen everyone for the first five minutes on a call, switch off all cameras

    - unless it is a training session or for some reason you really need everyone to be on camera
    - Video calls are draining because you must be in presentation mode all the time, as people can see you – ask me, I know!
    - We are not used to being on camera like a TV presenter, which comes with its own stressors, including the fact that you are desk-bound in this situation versus taking a phone call when you could be in the car or walking barefoot on the grass while you talk (you might have noticed that some people are pacers and often have their best thoughts while pacing)
    - Switch the camera on when you need to show your team something, or use it for social calls and check-ins
- Use asynchronous communication channels more and video less
    - Meetings on video often take place to make sure people are present, but are not strictly necessary if people are doing their jobs and providing relevant feedback where and when required
    - There are too many interruptions in workflow with too many meetings taking place
- The need for asynchronous communication means that employees need to know how to communicate clearly in writing when using text-based communication channels; this means they must be able to write and summarise well – much training is needed in this area
- Set specific times and create a specific place for water-cooler conversations and coffee breaks (we haven't been too successful at doing this online)
    - Don't make these part of a business meeting
    - Keep these separate
    - Create a channel within your group chat specifically for personal messages and news so that these don't clutter the business communication channels
- Everyone needs decent office equipment
    - In the office you have an ergonomic desk and chair; you should have the same at home
    - Companies may need to provide an allowance for this

  - A laptop stand or standing desk are also options
  - Noise-cancelling headphones with a microphone are useful if you don't have a dedicated office space
- A drinks/snacks allowance may be necessary to replace what would have been provided at work
- Respect personal time boundaries
  - One of the biggest learning curves relates to the start and end of the workday
  - While people may be playing catch-up with deep work after hours, this does not mean they need to be contactable or responsive
  - Changing WhatsApp accounts to business accounts can help with this, as you can create an automated message that says you will only reply to work messages during working hours
- Time management without being micromanaged is a skill set in itself
  - Help your team to learn how to plan and prioritise
  - Ensure that you and they know how to use project-management tools effectively
- Have face-to-face outings or retreats
  - As restrictions ease, face-to-face outings in small groups will be necessary; even a one-on-one walk-and-talk can be meaningful
  - These are important for human connection, re-bonding and trust-building

Takeaways for winning at home and life

- Create your own pros and cons list for working from home
  - This list helps you keep perspective
  - Share your list with your team or team leader
- Constantly strive to make things better for yourself and others, and be patient with yourself
  - Rome wasn't built in a day: it takes time to develop a new set of skills and grow comfortable with a new environment and expectations

   - You are likely already finding working from home easier to manage with a year of experience under your belt
- Be teachable
   - There is much to learn that will be helpful to you in a future where the work-from-anywhere scenario will be the reality for many – so embrace it
   - Be open to doing things differently; how you have always done things is not the only way
- Boundaries are important
   - Set up a routine to help you manage your time
   - This includes regular wake-up and bedtimes, exercise, mealtimes and relaxation time. If you have children, the importance of this will be discussed in more detail in Chapter 7
   - Your colleagues and management must respect your boundaries and so must your family, just as you must respect theirs
   - This scenario is new for everyone and we are all learning together; we will get better at it

Chapter 7

Working from home with kids

The most heartfelt wish most parents have expressed at my talks and workshops over the years has been, 'We wish we had more quality time with our children.' Now, by a bizarre twist of fate, as a result of a pandemic, many parents find themselves with their children 24/7 – and it completely overwhelms them. I call this the Covid-19 parenting paradox. Parents were not physically or psychologically prepared for the ongoing demands. Setting yourself up to work from home on purpose is one thing, but when you are forced to work from home, with children, without warning, that is another.[18]

Many reported that it was the first time they had spent so much uninterrupted time with their children, seen them in action, and really had the opportunity to get to know each other as a family on a different level. For others the situation has been overwhelming and extremely challenging, especially for families with very young children and those living and working in extremely small, crowded spaces. No matter how the experience has been for you, managing work-from-home overwhelm requires conscious effort and practise. It can be done, but it requires a new mindset and a dose of realism about life 24/7 with children, especially if you don't have a degree in child development!

MANAGE YOUR PANIC AND OVERWHELM: PRACTICAL HINTS

If you let fear and panic overwhelm you, you will freeze and not be any good to anyone. This is a time to learn how to be more mindful and to take time out for yourself, even if you can do so only in short bursts. If you don't look after yourself, you will not be able to look after your children or be productive and engaged with your work. Here are some practical suggestions for managing stress and panic:

- Sit quietly for five minutes two or three times a day and use the 4:7:8 breathing method to avoid letting your fears and stress hijack you. Close your eyes and put your hand on your belly button. To avoid shallow breathing, breathe into your hand on your belly button for a count of four, hold for a count of seven, and breathe out slowly for a count of eight. Do this at least five times or for five minutes and then you are ready to go again
- If you start to feel panicky or overwhelmed, get physical: doing ten star jumps, or if you have a staircase anywhere in the house, walking or running up and down the steps for a couple of minutes, will give your brain a good dose of endorphins – happiness hormones – and a much-needed oxygen boost
- Now would also be a good time to learn meditation skills. There are plenty of apps available with excellent meditations that can help alleviate your panic levels and centre your energy. When your energy is all over the place, so is everything else and everyone else around you

COMMUNICATION IS IMPERATIVE

Make sure you have a one-on-one meeting with your boss or manager to explain your current work-from-home situation if you have not already been consulted. Does your boss know how many children you have, how old they are and whether you have someone to help you with them? Without that information, you may land up like one of my clients who called me after watching my 'Reframing Covid-19 for You and Your Family' webinar for Henley Business School, who said, 'I am a working mom at home with an eighteen-month-old and a three-year-old and my boss thinks that because I am not commuting, now is an excellent time to give me a new project. He doesn't understand how difficult it is just to try to get my normal workload done under these circumstances, with constant interruptions and demands from my two small children! How do I tell him that taking on a new project right now will be impossible?'

Be realistic with yourself and your team. Don't overpromise and under-deliver, no matter how fearful you are of losing your job, as you will incapacitate yourself and be of use to no one. When we release our fears and ask for support, we find to our surprise that we can suddenly work much better. Fear truly can hijack your whole system.

LEARN HOW TO CHUNK

If you are working from home with kids, you must learn how to work around and with them, because they aren't going away any time soon. I believe we will continue to see a series of stop-starts, or a system of hybrid or rotational schooling, with some days a week spent at school and some online. This will mirror what is going to happen in companies who are talking about the future of work, even after restrictions are lifted, of employees only coming into the office two or three days a week and working from home the rest of the time.

Accept that you will have to get deep work, which needs focus and concentration, done before or after what used to be 'regular' work hours to accommodate your children's needs and schedules. This may mean working early in the morning before your children are awake, and at night after they have gone to bed. I'm afraid there is no quick fix here, unless you can employ an au pair or tutor to manage your children while you work. I have worked from home for twenty-five years and have had children at different ages and stages throughout that time, so I know how frustrating it is when you don't have any continuity and have to fit your work around your kids. This is real life and you will get used to it over time. As your children mature they will need your supervision less, freeing up your time. I will never forget how much uninterrupted work I managed to do once my youngest went to preschool for three hours a day, and then, when he went to primary school for five hours a day, and again when he started extramural activities in earnest in Grade 2 and I suddenly had even more time to get things done and could commit to more in my career.

You will need to do what I call 'chunking': working hard, fast and with razor-sharp focus for sixty to ninety minutes at a time, once or twice a day. That's about all you can expect if you have children under the age of seven. You will learn how to have fantastic focus, because you won't have time for a redo and have to be productive in less time than usual, because that is all the time you have. During the day, you need to learn how to work in short sprints to feel a sense of completion and progress. You might want to employ a back-to-basics technique called the Pomodoro Technique. I've been doing a version of it for years and never knew it had a name, but here it is!

EFFICIENCY USING THE POMODORO TECHNIQUE

I love simple solutions. Francesco Cirillo developed the Pomodoro Technique, which has helped millions make friends with time and increase their productivity. Its name is based on those original kitchen timers that were shaped like a tomato ('pomodoro' is Italian for tomato). All you'll need for it is a timer and a task to complete. Beyond that, no special apps, books or tools are required. Here's how to get started with the Pomodoro Technique, in five steps:

Step 1: Choose a task to be accomplished
Step 2: Set your pomodoro (timer) to twenty-five minutes
Step 3: Work on the task until the pomodoro rings, then put a check mark on a sheet of paper
Step 4: Take a short break (five minutes)
Step 5: After every fourth pomodoro session, take a longer break (fifteen to thirty minutes).

The longer break, I find, is both the biggest challenge and the most important discipline. While we want to keep going when we are on a roll, we also need to give our brains a break to cope over the long haul and to maintain sufficiently high levels of creative and problem-solving ability. A longer break is anything from fifteen to thirty minutes, before you start the next twenty-five-minute work session. Repeat the process a few times over the course of a workday, and you will feel a sense of accomplishment and progress, while also doing so in a way that is healthy for you. The longer breaks can be used to kill a few birds with one stone:

- make a cup of coffee
- eat lunch
- spend some time with your children on a regular basis throughout the day
- get out the ingredients for supper
- set the next activity for your children to do while you do your next pomodoro session.

Discipline and boundaries are at the heart of the Pomodoro Technique. If you are distracted for some reason by a colleague, a child, a meeting, or an emergency, you either end the pomodoro (saving your work and starting a new session later), or you postpone the distraction until you have completed your pomodoro session. If you can postpone the distraction, Cirillo suggests using the 'inform, negotiate and call back' strategy:[19]

- *Inform* the other (or distracting) party that you're working on something right now
- *Negotiate* a time when you can get back to them about the distracting issue in a timely manner
- *Schedule* that follow-up immediately
- *Call back* the other party when your pomodoro is complete and you're ready to tackle their issue.

If you have a child over seven who can tell the time, you can make them timekeeper for the day with a bell or whistle they can ring or blow when the alarm goes off to indicate when you reach the end of a pomodoro session. Get them involved in your productivity plan. It will give them a role to play and a sense of control at a time when things are feeling out of control.

This simple technique (you may have found others) can help you spend less time on what you must do, and more time on what you want to do. Give it a try! Or use the technique as a team or a family. I think kids will get into the fun of renaming work or school 'Let's do another pomodoro!' A sense of humour is part of resilience.

PLAYING TAG TEAM WITH THE CHILDREN

If you have children at home with you, the ideal situation is to have another adult around when you have to work, even if they have to work too. This means taking turns working and looking after or supervising playtime, schoolwork and naps, much like a relay. Who is on your team, sharing your home and workspace? Your teammates might be:

- a spouse or partner
- an au pair
- a tutor
- a grandparent
- a domestic helper
- other families in the same position as you.

I am seeing a shift here too, with parents who made use of an au pair's services opting for tutors in the work-from-home/school-from-home scenario. Times are changing, so we need to use and develop support structures that work for us.

CREATE VISUAL CUES THAT INDICATE YOU ARE IN WORK MODE

Depending on the physical limitations of your home, you can do more or less of this, but children need visual cues to remind themselves that you are working and cannot be interrupted. For very small children, this is difficult.

- Create a dedicated workspace if you can
- If your office has a door, you can close the door to show that you are working
- If you are in an open-plan situation, put masking tape down on the floor to demarcate your workspace or place a work jacket or a sign that says 'working' on a chair when you are working. It means 'don't cross this line and interrupt me'
- You may find that dressing for work gets you more into the zone. It can also work as a visual cue to your children that you are in work mode now. Some children may feel more in routine to dress in their school uniform for the morning, even though they are doing school at home
- Consider having a wacky work hat that you all put on when it is work time. Although this is something I wouldn't do because I get 'hat hair' that I wouldn't be able to revive before I have to go on camera, you might find it works for you. It signals to your children that you can't be disturbed until you take the hat off. Remember to take it off for your next on-camera meeting, though – or leave it on for a laugh; it will make a great conversation-starter!

ROUTINE AND PLANNING

Routine is essential, and it's wise to spend some time working out a routine that will work best for you and your family with its own unique needs. Routine is about the order of things more than the times when things will occur. Keep the order the same, even if you are half an hour out – this way everyone can stay sane, because things remain predictable. Predictability is key: you will stress less that bath time didn't happen at 6 p.m. exactly, and focus on the fact that it happened and that supper happened after that – sometimes, things like getting your children to sleep at night are achievements in themselves.

Whether you are working from home or the office, a family routine communicates these basics:

- This is what we do
- This is when we do it
- This is how we do it
- These are your limits
- This is what is expected of you
- This is what is expected of me.

A flexible mindset is essential when absorbing change and coping with disruption. If something is not working for you after you have given it a good go, then change it up and see what happens. Routines will also change when children are on holiday, even if you are having a staycation at home. Draw up a daily schedule for your family that incorporates your workload and what they need to get through, depending on whether they are on holiday or in term time.

Planning

On the topic of planning: a little bit of planning can go a long way, especially with younger children between two and seven years of age.

Pre-pack a box or little plastic suitcase with activities for your child to do every morning while you are working – things they can age-appropriately do by themselves, and to keep them busy when it is pomodoro time. Make sure this suitcase only gets taken out at this time. They can play with other toys and games the rest of the time. Ring the changes every day and include:

- something to play with
- something to colour in or draw with
- something that will fascinate them
- something to read (for young children, board books, 'feely' books, sound books, and so on).

Pack a lunchbox for each child every morning as you would for school, then you don't have to field constant requests for food and drinks throughout the morning. The lunchbox is a visual, tactile and taste cue that they are self-sufficient, and they don't need you.

BE SURE TO PLAY

I know this sounds crazy at a time when you are barely surviving working from home while also managing your children's needs 24/7, but the gift children bring is the opportunity to press the pause button and stop for a while to shift yourself into a more playful zone. If you can combine this once or twice a day with your longer pomodoro breaks, you will be investing in your relationship with your children in a way that will pay dividends for years to come. At the same time you will be bringing your stress levels down, so it's a win–win. Just make sure you choose quick games to play when you take a play break. There are many fabulous games around that take only ten to fifteen minutes to play, so be on the lookout for those. Read my toy reviews on my website at www.nikkibush.com for my current list of highly recommended games and toys.

Make sure these play breaks are filled with hugs, and give your children your full attention to fill up their emotional cups. Be proactive. They will be less needy, and interruptions will decline because they know they are important to you and they trust that you will show up for them. They will not need to resort to negative attention-seeking behaviour – whingeing, whining and complaining, or getting themselves into trouble – to get your attention. You can find many quick and easy 'boredom-buster' activities on my website, including science, craft and cooking activities that require only a little of your time and normal household objects or ingredients. These activities will capture your child's attention and imagination, making you a parenting hero (despite also working like a demon).

INVITE YOUR KIDS TO DO THE CHORES WITH YOU

An essential element of parenting on the run is to get your children to help out with doing the household chores.[20] Every household has them – they are the glue that keeps family life together. They have to be done, and getting children involved from an early age (I recommend from age three) has multiple benefits: from teaching essential life skills, to passing on the baton of responsibility and encouraging independence. Interestingly, children under twelve want to get good at doing what they see you doing every day.

Parents tend to avoid inviting their kids to help with the chores, believing it's more expedient and less messy to do it themselves. This can result in parents getting into a habit of serving their children, and kids growing up helpless. If you leave it too late, children believe that they aren't good enough to help, which can lead to a crisis of confidence or result in entitlement and laziness. Doing chores together teaches kids important stuff, gives you the opportunity to praise and encourage them, and fosters a feeling of belonging and togetherness. Do not think of chores as wasted time but as an investment in precious quality time, and an opportunity for future-proofing your child and assisting you (and your children) with work–life integration. More about this in Chapter 8.

PAIR UP THEIR SCREEN TIME WITH YOUR WORK

Start using your children's screen time strategically, especially during the school holidays or if you have young children who cannot do things on their own, or you don't have additional adult help. Of course, children need us to impose limits on their screen time, otherwise they would just lie in front of a screen all day and do nothing else. It takes less energy and effort to do screen-based activities than it does to play, and it numbs the pain of being without you. However, we also know that it is a great babysitter when you must get things done, as your children will sit still, not make a mess and won't interrupt you. Bingo!

If you can be disciplined about this, you can create an agreement with them that they can be on a screen – for example, TV or gaming – for a set number of pomodoros until you take your long break after four pomodoros. This approach requires discipline, though, in that you must be able to be with them during that long break. You are the prize! And when you take your five-minute breaks, they have to take them too. In that time you can get refreshments or do a bit of exercise with your kids – even if it's just rope skipping or star jumps. We have to activate our systems and wake them up from being sedentary, for the good of our bodies and minds.

TYPICAL OUTLINE FOR A DAILY ROUTINE

Wake up
Shower and get dressed
Eat breakfast

Morning work session

- Parents need to work
- While the parents work, small children do activities that are learning-oriented (educational games and toys, puzzles, reading, online educational games, construction toys, colouring in, and so on), while older children go to school or get busy with online learning
- Schedule some screen time for your children if you have to be on an uninterrupted call/in a meeting – that way they won't interrupt you
- Younger children up to three years will need almost constant supervision if they are not sleeping
- From age three to six, children will be able to focus on something on their own for about ten minutes; at this age they generally need an adult around to intervene, support and encourage them from time to time to keep them going
- From age six to nine, they should be able to concentrate for about fifteen to twenty minutes at a time

Lunchtime

- If you are at home, you will need a break – and your kids need to see you
- Try to take your lunch break with them
- If possible, switch off your devices for the duration of your lunch break
- Children need to experience you being fully present, even if it is only for fifteen to twenty minutes

Afternoon work session

- Parents need to work
- Children can do fun, play-based activities:
  - Arts and crafts
  - Science experiments
  - Cooking
  - Cycling
  - Visiting the park
  - Limited screen time.

If there is any possibility of you being able to take part in something for a short while, that is great. If not, try to do something with them at the end of the day or after supper. Even swimming, exercising or bathing together works a treat

Chore time

- Feeding the pets

- Closing curtains
- Cooking
- Laying the table
- Folding washing, washing up dishes, and so on
- Bath time for younger children (bath time is a powerful multisensory signal that the day is coming to an end)

Supper time
- Switch off devices
- Be fully present with each other
- Have conversations
- Catch up on the day

Family time
- Watch a series together
- Play a game together
- Brush teeth
- Story time for younger children
- Bedtime

For more information on working from home with children, read Chapter 7.

Takeaways for winning at work

- Be flexible: try different things and find out what works best for you and your home team in collaboration with your work team
- If you are leading a team:
  - Get to know your team members and their home situations in as much detail as you can, so that you can support them in experimenting with what works and what doesn't
  - Have empathy for everyone in this work-from-home experiment, even yourself!
  - A breathing exercise such as the 4:7:8 breathing method described on page 63 is a great way to start a meeting to get everyone 'into the room', so to speak, and to help them to separate from what they were doing beforehand

- Just as a school-from-home scenario cannot be a mirror image of a normal school day in a controlled educational environment, so a work-from-home situation is not a mirror image of work in a controlled office environment; it requires reinvention, reimagining and constant tweaking to make it work
- Collaborate and communicate with each other to create the most workable situation you can; aim for workable – not perfect
- Remember that the IT environment is iterative: products go to market before they are perfect and the bugs are worked out along the way; we have to adopt a similar experimental mindset in the work-from-home situation

Takeaways for winning at home and life

- Learn how to tango with your children: there are different steps and different tempos to master, but you must be up for the dance
- Children are now part of the equation; learn how to work with and around them
- Planning takes time, but it is worth it; I call this Mission Control, and Sunday night was my favourite time to plan the week with my children when they were younger
- Remember that a routine refers to the order of things: if your timing is slightly out, don't beat yourself up – simply keep the order the same, and you and your family will stay sane
- Have a backup plan for when things go wrong or something unexpected happens – it's called plan B
    - Call for backup support, if needed – someone who could take your kids out of the house for a walk, or to the park for an hour while you regroup or get something essential done
    - Plan B might involve extra screen time, but don't make it your default
    - Go for workable – not perfect; good enough is good enough
    - For families to work there needs to be more connection and less perfection
    - Children need your emotional presence more than they need

gifts; this means giving them the gift of your time, which you can do even on the run and in small doses

- A short game here, doing chores together there, reading a bedtime story, exercising together and eating meals together – these little pockets of time all add up

Chapter 8

Empathy for parents

Working from home has become the new norm and is easier for some than for others. Without doubt, logistically it is easier for those without children or who have much older children. Emotionally, however, it may be harder from a loneliness perspective when work and life are taking place in the same physical space continuously without company. Do spare a special thought, though, for those with babies, preschoolers or young primary-school children who need constant supervision or assistance.

When you have set yourself up on purpose to work from home with kids, you put things in place: a separate office, a house that is big enough, childcare assistance and school. However, the pandemic lockdown put people in a position where these preparations were largely absent, forcing work-from-home parents to work under demanding and less-than-ideal conditions for productivity and performance.

This chapter focuses on the realities of people who are working from home with children and the need for a deeper understanding of your team members and yourself.

The daily reality of working from home with kids means that team members need to do any deep work for business that requires focus and attention to detail before the children wake up in the morning and after they go to bed at night. During their children's waking hours they will only be able to handle small tasks in short bursts, unless they have domestic help available or they have a partner or spouse who is also working from home and can work and do childcare or supervision in relays with this person.

Employees who have children at home will be more exhausted than ever, as they haven't had much time to adjust to their new working and living conditions. Right now, employees are feeling drained by the general feeling of panic and fear that is everywhere. Even a year into the pandemic, many questions will be running through their heads all the time:

- Will the world go back to normal?
- What will the world look like then?
- Will my company still be in business?
- Will I still have a job?
- Will my salary be cut?
- How long will I have to keep on working from home?
- How long will my children be at home and not at school?
- Will I or a member of my family become ill?

Many employees who are now working from home don't have dedicated home offices with doors that close. They are having to work in their bedrooms or in common family areas, which means they don't have privacy or guaranteed peace and quiet. It is exhausting. I know this, because I was in a similar position for the first few months of lockdown: I had to turn my open-plan lounge into my office-cum-TV studio for presenting virtually. My workspace was right in the centre of my home. Pre-pandemic my eldest son was overseas, and my youngest was away at university. During the first lockdown they were both home in our small rented cluster house. (We had to sell our large home of twenty-three years after my husband's death.)

I had endless distractions and interruptions – from gaming and TV to someone making a meal in the kitchen or walking past and wanting to chat. When I needed to present live on camera, everyone had to shut up, go to their rooms, and not use the internet to give me priority to work and earn a living. Stress levels were sky-high. This is real life for many working parents right now.

UNDERSTANDING YOUR EMPLOYEES AND TEAM MEMBERS

If you are a business owner, employer or team manager, here are some insights to help you understand how to make the best of the situation and to journey more effectively together with your team.

- It is key that you know your individual employees.
    - How many children are they managing at home?
    - What ages are the children?

  - Do they have live-in adult assistance or domestic help at this time?
  - Are they a single parent?
  - Do they have a spouse or partner who will be sharing the space with them?
  - Will that person be able to share childcare responsibilities?
- For people who previously spent only two to three hours with their children on a normal workday, spending twenty-four hours a day together is challenging
- While most working parents usually carry a mantle of guilt because they don't think they spend enough time with their children, now that they have been given more time with their children, albeit under the strangest of circumstances, they are pretty freaked out by it because of the implications for their productivity and not being used to spending so much time with their kids; this is the Covid-19 parenting paradox
- Your team members are working with new schedules, new systems, new working environments (often without a dedicated home office) and new forms of interference
- New interferences will include:
  - children
  - device-sharing with children who are doing online schooling or with a spouse or partner
  - poor bandwidth or no data
- Emotionally, they are also in a state of
  - shock
  - fear
  - panic
  - overwhelm
  - grief
- Parents who are working remotely from home will have *much* longer days than usual while they adjust to a new rhythm and routine, and they will be tired
- Their days will not run in a straightforward, linear fashion: they will be filled with many interruptions that neither you nor they can necessarily control
- Parents will be doing their work in chunks, often getting up to do it

early before the children wake, or staying up late to do it after the children have gone to sleep. Having worked from home with children for twenty-five years, I know this for a fact. Many of my colleagues who have also run businesses from home (some up to medium-sized enterprises) attest to the same. This is just the way it is.

UNDERSTANDING CHILDREN

Businesses, by and large, are not built around the health of family life and children's developmental needs. But perhaps one of the positive spinoffs of the pandemic will be that the human resources playbook will be rewritten to be more supportive of work–life integration. Here are some high-level insights to bear in mind when you are working with remote-working parents with kids that will make you more empathetic as a boss or a colleague.

Children are flesh and blood, not robots

Children are not robots or computers who can be programmed to run on their own or not interrupt their parents while they work. Children are also feeling frightened and anxious at this time. They will need more attention than usual from their parents – their routine has been turned upside down; they can't see their friends; often they won't be going to school and are stuck at home with parents who are stressed, need to work and are not much fun to be with.

Children have shorter concentration spans than adults

We must be realistic about a child's ability to concentrate and get on with doing things by themselves. This is vitally important to know, as it is rarely taken into consideration by employers or the parents they employ. It is the source of much frustration, which could be diffused with a little more understanding. An understanding of children's different ages and stages is useful here.

REALITY CHECK:

Children acquire about a minute and a half's concentration for every year of their life – they learn how to concentrate on activities for longer periods than that with adult interaction at home and at school to keep them focused.

Now that you have fallen off your chair, get back on again and continue reading:

- Children from birth to three years will need almost constant supervision unless they are sleeping
- Children from three to five years of age may be able to entertain themselves for five to fifteen minutes at a time (age- and skill-dependent), without supervision, if you are lucky
- Under-fives need a lot of attention; this is not abnormal, because they need stimulation and environmental feedback to make sense of the world; they will also be very busy. It's called childhood – not necessarily ADD!
- Only by Grade 1 can children focus for a full fifteen to twenty minutes on an activity without much supervision; even then, this would have to be a game or school activity they have already mastered, not something new
- From six to nine years onwards, children are able to entertain themselves for longer periods. They will need some help doing schoolwork from home, and you will need to assist them with setting up their workspace and settling them into an activity or help out as the need arises, which it will
- Parents with children between nine and twelve years of age will be able to settle their children with an activity (play or academic) for about twenty to thirty minutes at a time, but they will still need some direction and supervision – although they will interrupt their parents less
- Teens will be able to entertain themselves and should be able to manage their academic timetable with much less help from their parents, although they may still get stuck. Parents will find themselves in a supervisory role here: they will stress about monitoring their teens' need to socialise online and the possibility that they might overdose on screen time, and may feel like they are in the dark if their child is not communicating with them.

As schools will not necessarily reopen immediately or fully after various stages of lockdown, or will close and reopen in between infection surges, children will be in a state of limbo for the foreseeable future. Just as you get used to a change, things may shift overnight. These changes require adaptability and flexibility from all parties, including employers. Without a doubt, working parents have had to take on a greater role in their children's education during the pandemic, adding to their workloads, especially if they are unfamiliar with guiding their child's academic journey. This may be the first global pandemic we have experienced, but it will not be the last.

Parents are not used to being their child's teachers. There is a huge difference between introducing new concepts and consolidating learning around concepts that children have already been taught in a classroom environment. Children in the foundation phase (between five and nine years of age) represent one of the biggest challenges for both parents and teachers alike, as much of the academic learning in these years should ideally be concrete, hands-on and experiential. Learning through discovery rather than instruction is preferable, and there is only so much a teacher can achieve on a screen, or in a socially distanced classroom. The interaction limitations of on-screen instruction go against the very nature of children's need to move and explore their world.

Although in their new role, parents are not the teacher, they are now their children's guide, and they will feel anxious about not having all the answers, or not being able to motivate their child to complete work – which is often a stress response on the part of the child.

As you can gauge from the above, working at home with children, especially if you have to home-school too, is demanding and stressful and will take some time to get used to. Parents now have multiple roles to fulfil. Many are also not used to being with their children for such extended periods of time, which is an adjustment all on its own.

WHAT ABOUT YOU, THE TEAM LEADER OR MANAGER?

If you are in the same boat as your team members – working remotely and parenting 24/7 too – then you are in a better position to be empathetic and understanding. If you are a single parent, or not a parent yet, lockdown and working remotely will have different challenges for you as you try to lead people who are being pulled in many different directions while you might simply want to get on with your job.

Regardless of the situation in which you find yourself, you are ultimately responsible for leading your team members to fulfil their key performance indicators and deliver for the business to survive. You are under extreme pressure to make it all happen, to find a way to make this extraordinary situation work. Acknowledge that:

- Everything has changed
- Everyone is in a state of transition, including you
- You are going through this too and you can share your own lived experience with your team – it makes you real
- You need to take care of yourself so that your cup is full, enabling you to continue filling the cups of others
- You cannot work from a place of emptiness
- You need to lead now, more than ever before; your personal leadership and team leadership are needed, both at home and at work
- You must tap into how you are feeling to have empathy with others
- Don't deny your feelings and your fears – rather find a way to work through them and with them; use them as your teachers and guides, to not only think your way through this crisis, but also to act intuitively and stay in touch with your feelings
- Make use of the services of a counsellor or coach at this time if you need to – we all need cheerleaders and guides from time to time. Like a psychologist sees a supervisor to offload with them on a regular basis, team leaders and managers may need to do the same to decompress and not take on their team members' stresses personally
- You need to take the time to redefine your team's goal(s), even if they are interim goals, until the Covid-19 mists clear and you can see a bit further down the track
- While empathy is important, you need to support your team members to discover and create their own solutions. Empower them to develop their problem-solving muscle instead of defaulting to rescuing them. In fact, why not make this part of your team culture at work and at home? This is leadership.

I hope that if you are managing a team you can see that the challenges and demands that your team members with children are currently facing should not be underestimated or swept aside. You will need to be patient and tolerant as people settle into their new spaces. You will need to be empathetic and reasonable, or your team members will crack under the enormous pressure they are experiencing. They need support and coaching as to how best to handle their workload in the context of their individual circumstances, and how to maintain boundaries and still feel a sense of growth and satisfaction in the face of much frustration and adjustment.

Yes, you are taking on a parenting role here, in a sense, but I have always believed that this is part of the role of a team leader or manager. Team leaders, much like parents, should raise up their team members to become independent, resourceful and resilient. Flexibility and adaptability are being called for in bucketloads right now.

Takeaways for winning at work

- Be aware of who in your team is a parent and what support they have
- Find out how old their children are and bear in mind the attention spans at play and how these will affect each employee
- What kind of support can your organisation offer? Do you have an employee assistance programme (financial, legal, medical and psychological advice and support)? Bear in mind that 68 per cent of people would prefer to talk to a robot rather than their manager about stress and anxiety at work, and 80 per cent of people are open to having a robot as a therapist or counsellor, according to the March 2021 issue of *Forbes Africa*. My bet is that staff will worry that if they are honest about their struggles, their manager may hold it against them when it comes to performance appraisals and promotions. This is something to think about and address
- If certain perks no longer apply in the work-from-home scenario, perhaps the money can be redirected to pay for childcare and additional support at home? We must start thinking differently about what needs to happen to keep our businesses running under new circumstances
- Help your team members to future-proof themselves for business continuity and their own job security
- As an individual, you need to learn how to play this new game as effectively as you can to bring your productivity up to speed

Takeaways for winning at home and life

- Look how resourceful and flexible you are becoming! These characteristics are great X factors for success in a changing world – and employers value them
- Look how you are taking on self-leadership: this skill will stand you in good stead for any disruption that lies ahead, something that even the World Economic Forum has highlighted in their *The Future of Jobs Report* mentioned in Chapter 2
- Take on the challenge of changing the way you think about how things ought to be and be resourceful in the present
- This is the time to re-examine and drop assumptions about work and life and the myth of work–life balance
- Have a sense of humour
- Forgive yourself when things don't always work out according to plan. I learnt this the hard way as a self-confessed list queen, discovering very quickly as a working parent that the concept of Supermom or Superdad was a myth: children need everyday heroes who show up for them consistently, not perfectly
- Watch your hours – it's tempting to overwork to overcompensate, but you need to develop a long-haul mentality; this is a marathon, not a sprint

Chapter 9

Raise your impact on a screen

The Covid-19 pandemic has seen billions of people being sent home to work remotely, via a screen. This trend will continue into the foreseeable future and may even become the norm. This means more meetings and presentations are being done from behind a webcam without normal access to the multitude of human visual and non-verbal cues that we have in face-to-face meetings. How to improve your virtual impact on a screen is an issue everyone should be addressing.

We have to find ways to be influential, command respect, keep calm and maintain authority in this virtual space. How to raise your presence in front of the webcam is now a challenge every businessperson, presenter or educator who wants to connect strongly and be taken seriously must consider.

As a professional speaker and 2020/21 president of the Johannesburg chapter of the Professional Speakers Association of Southern Africa, I present webinars and run online meetings every day. I also coach clients on how to raise their presence, impact on and engage in virtual meeting spaces. There are some basics many people miss that would help to lift their game enormously before they need to do anything costly, such as upgrading their microphone or webcam.

SOME COMMON MISTAKES AND HOW TO FIX THEM

The most common mistakes people make in online presentations relate to the chosen camera angle, strange backdrops, unsuitable lighting and awkward body position. These are simple to fix.

Camera angle

- You only have to watch the news on TV to see how most people get this very wrong. Their laptops are too low, so they are seen looking down their noses at the audience who, in turn, are entertained by a nostril view, which is generally not very attractive

- The easy way to remedy this is to place your laptop on a box or a pile of books so that the camera is at eye level
- Work with the angle of the laptop to avoid giving the audience a view of your ceiling and only a little of your face. Your face should be in the centre of the frame
- Avoid looking at your own face or that of the person you are speaking to. Instead, look straight into the camera lens if you really want to connect with the other person. This is probably one of the most difficult things to get right, as we tend to be drawn to other people's faces and most people are not used to being on camera
- Stick something bright, like a sticker, near the camera lens to remind you where you should be looking
- Clean your camera lens regularly to avoid a blurry picture.

Backdrop

- Avoid sitting with a bright window or slatted Venetian blinds behind you, as the viewer's eye is instantly drawn to the light (or you might appear as an angel with a halo around you)
- If you are sitting in front of a bookshelf or any form of shelving, make sure it is neat and tidy. The eye is drawn to things that are not lined up or are skew
- Make sure you do not have a plant growing out of your ear or any part of your head
- Remove pictures from the wall behind you if they are distracting.
- Try to position yourself with as little visual clutter behind you as possible; a plain curtain or a plain wall is usually good
- Virtual backgrounds work well on MS Teams, and you don't need to use a green screen. However, if you are using an app like Zoom, you will need very good lighting and a green screen (blue or green fabric) behind you to make it work, or you will end up with a fuzzy green halo around you – and when you move your hands, they will make green streaks on

the screen. It is generally not advisable to use a virtual background, unless you have a very professional set-up.

Lighting

- Your face needs to be well lit. I can't tell you how many people are literally in the dark and you can't see their eyes or their mouths at all. This is not conducive to connection and communication
- You need, at the very least, two sources of light coming towards you. If you are sitting at a laptop, two bedside lamps with bendy heads positioned on either side of your laptop, in front of you, at 45 degrees to each other, will help a lot
- Play with the positioning of the lamps to create a good look and feel. Ask someone to help you, and check out the result with others on the other side of your screen
- Once you have your light sources in front of you, there might be a shadow on the wall or curtain behind you, which you may have to dissipate by positioning a lamp without a lampshade on the floor behind you
- You may need to diffuse the light by placing a piece of wax paper over the light source with laundry pegs (think of photographic lighting), especially if you wear glasses, as you want to avoid the reflection of the light source. I wear glasses, and this is a tough challenge
- Inexpensive ring lights also work well (unless you wear glasses)
- Watch out for the moving sun on your windows: you may need to reposition yourself depending on the time of day if it is an important meeting in which you need to show up with maximum credibility.

Sound

- You want to come across as clearly as possible
- A cellphone hands-free set plugged into your computer will provide better sound than if you simply talk into the computer's built-in microphone
- Watch out for echo in a room. To avoid an echo, close your curtains, place duvets and blankets on hard surfaces and put towels over mirrors to stop your voice from bouncing back. It makes an enormous difference.
- Avoid squeaky chairs
- Make sure your pets are safe and won't interrupt your meeting. My son

opened his parrot's cage while I was in a virtual EXCO meeting during lockdown. Guess where said parrot landed? On my head. (Although I admit that this made for a memorable meeting!)

- You can also purchase inexpensive plug-and-play microphones. Have some fun – go out and test them. They can make a huge difference to how you come across online. Your microphone is even more important than your camera.

Body position

- Do you sit or stand?
- Most people sit for the duration of meetings. However, when you are speaking there is a limit to how much you can move your body to express yourself. I sit for long meetings but stand for presentations. There is more power, energy and authority when you stand, and much more scope for movement sideways, forwards and backwards. You can use your space better than when you are seated
- Remember that you need to adjust the position and height of your laptop when you decide to stand
- You may want to invest in a standing desk or keep a number of boxes of different heights handy. I used the box option for a year and have since graduated to a mechanical desk I can raise and lower as needed.

Initially, don't worry about buying special equipment; get the basics right – you will be amazed at the difference it can make.

How you appear on a screen, how comfortable you feel while you are 'under a magnifying glass' and how well you make direct eye contact will go a long way towards raising your presence and your impact on-screen without having to invest in expensive state-of-the-art equipment.

Takeaways for winning at work

- Small changes can make a big difference
- Ask someone to evaluate your appearance on a screen and give you feedback – you don't know what you don't know!
- Make changes to boost your confidence and credibility

- Aim to raise your likeability and trust scores online
- Because you are more comfortable and confident, you will increase your influence with these micro-changes
- Learn how to share your humanity across the airwaves – make the other person feel as if you are speaking directly to them and really connecting
- Remember that eye contact is essential!

Takeaways for winning at home and life

- The confidence you develop in front of the camera will follow you into your home life
- Use the tricks you learnt for working on-screen in your social interactions with friends and family online – you might be surprised at how this improves your interactions

PART 3

BUILDING YOUR RESILIENCE MUSCLE

About six months after my husband's death I received an email from a client who had been observing my process of working through grief and getting up again, who wrote, 'This challenge didn't bury you, it planted you like a seed.' It was sobering and motivating at the same time. It was sent from someone who knew me in my professional capacity. He had probably been in the audience at one of my talks and was on my mailing list for this reason. I had no idea who he was. Receiving an objective message from someone outside my inner circle was extremely affirming, and it confirmed that I was indeed working through my Collateral Damage Repair Process©.

We can choose to be buried by the damage of disruption, or we can allow ourselves to be vulnerable, to step into a process without knowing where it will lead us, and be broken open, unleashing potential and possibilities we never even knew were there.

This is the adventure I alluded to regarding the upside of trauma and disruption, which can be seen as a gift. Often, the more seismic the disruption, the less you have to lose if you allow the breaking-open process to happen, because you are forced to let go of life as it was, as well as some of your perceptions and ideals. You are able to entertain other options and possibilities that you never would or could have had before. It is an opportunity for rebirth. It's a reinvention gap. But not everyone takes it.

In my mid-thirties I damaged a third disc in my lower back in a Pilates class (the first two were damaged in my first pregnancy). It was another What If™ moment in my life, one in which physical disruption opened a sea of positive change for me that I could never have anticipated. I was overwhelmed by pain and in constant agony and could barely walk. My chiropractor sent me off to orthopaedic and neurosurgeons, who declared that I needed a spinal fusion, but I was far too young – I should go home and pretend I had had the procedure. That involved wearing a corset, not sitting for four months and spending most of that time lying down.

With my young sons being two-and-a-half and six years old at the time, the thought of being incapacitated was impractical and inconceivable. I remember sitting in my car after paying for the specialist appointment to read the MRI scans and phoning my mom. I told her, 'I just paid a fortune to be told to go home and heal myself!' To say I was furious was an understatement.

However, looking back, this was a moment when I chose to disrupt myself on purpose. I chose the road less travelled. I took the advice I had been given, lay down and surrendered. They had passed on the baton of responsibility to me to find my own way to heal and adjust my life so that I would not have a fully fused spine by the age of fifty. Was it rough? Did it require patience and perseverance? Did it require resourcefulness? Yes, absolutely. I chose to see those four months as a healing crisis, as an investment in my future, a forced sabbatical. The full journey to stability and strength took three years, and I am always still at risk of re-injuring my back.

What was the gift that came from making that choice to stop, and opening that door in this situation? It was in the stopping, the being quiet, and having time to contemplate and reflect on what was important to me. How could I do my work and life differently to make it more workable in the future with a compromised back? Friends and family were amazing – fetching and carrying my children and taking me to therapy (the only time I ever sat was in a car when going to various forms of physical and alternative therapy ten minutes away). I had to learn how to stand and walk all over again – back to basics, so I wouldn't hurt myself in the future. Experts estimate that modern medicine will allow us to live for a long time, so you have to do what you can to keep yourself mobile and strong. Your body and health are important assets for future-proofing yourself.

While I didn't stop working, this disruption made me do my work much more slowly and very differently. I subcontracted some of it out (a big thing for me at the time). The rest I did standing up with my laptop on boxes on the kitchen counter to make sure everything was ergonomically workable and didn't injure me further. I would work for short periods of fifteen to twenty minutes at a time and then lie down for an hour. (I was already unwittingly using the Pomodoro Technique I described in Chapter 7.) It was a slow process, but I was moving forward, and I was still in business. Over time I worked for longer and lay down for shorter periods.

During the four months of pretending to have had a spinal fusion, I spent many hours lying in traction on the floor of our bedroom (the floor was actually pretty comfortable). I spent the time reading, reflecting, praying and meditating – not something a busy working mother with two young children would normally have much time to do. In the stillness I really heard the call, one that had been spoken out loud to me many times and which I had ignored. That was to find my own voice. I took the courageous step to stand up and speak professionally for the first time under my own name, not on behalf of the company for which I consulted. By stopping, I was able to connect my head and heart and *feel* my way forward instead of *thinking* my way forward, which so many of us in today's busy world are prone to doing.

As it turns out, the surgeons' refusal to operate and throwing the ball into my court taught me many lessons about resilience. My anger and frustration turned into determination and perseverance. I changed the way I did things, and life did not end. In fact, I developed a whole new lease on life.

In Elizabeth Lesser's incredible book *Broken Open*, which was one of only two books that made sense to me in the depths of my grief after my husband's death, she talks about surrendering to a time of great difficulty, allowing the pain to break us open, and then being reborn – stronger, wiser and kinder. I have found this insight to be true. There comes a time when we have to stop fighting and trying to control the uncontrollable. We need to surrender and accept where we find ourselves and work with what is.

I agree with Lesser that we can reproduce ourselves from the shattered pieces of a difficult time:

> Our lives ask us to die and to be reborn every time we confront change – change within ourselves and change in our world. When we descend all the way down to the bottom of a loss, and dwell patiently with an open heart, in the darkness and pain, we can bring back up with us the sweetness of life and the exhilaration of inner growth. When there is nothing left to lose, we find the true self – the self that is whole, the self that is enough, the self that no longer looks to others for definition, or completion, or anything but companionship on the journey.[21]

Allowing oneself to be broken open by a situation or circumstance is not a show of weakness but of strength. When you stop dwelling on 'it shouldn't be happening to me' and accept that it is, you are opening up to growth and rebirth. While you don't know what might lie beyond the mists, and the burden of what you carry may be heavy, you can also believe that it is full of potential. Our hope lies in accepting life as it is and not as we wish it could be. Nothing good or bad lasts forever.

Experience definitely counts. I am so grateful that I had twenty-five or more years of deep personal development work under my belt when my husband was killed. I had tools *and* fifty years of life experience that my eighteen- and twenty-three-year-old sons didn't have. This enabled me to cope in a very different way (note that I did not say 'better') for two reasons: I had more perspective, and I had grown my resilience muscle more than they had over the years of my life.

As terrible as things were in the two years following the tragedy, I could say to myself with conviction that this too shall pass. I could remember other trying times in my life when I had survived and overcome, although nothing was quite as universally shattering and disruptive as the situation I was going through then. But it helped bolster my courage at the time.

As you read this section, I want to invite you to contemplate some of the difficult moments you have been through in your life and what they taught you about yourself. How are you stronger for them, no matter how tough they might have been? How have you adapted to risk and adversity, to multiple challenges, to failure? In her TEDWomen talk from 2017, 'The Gift and Power of Emotional Courage', psychologist Susan David made this powerful statement: 'Courage is not the absence of fear; courage is fear walking.'[22] Where have you shown courage through change?

Chapter 10

Taking responsibility in disruption

We all experience What If™ moments – from marital hiccups to full-blown relationship breakdowns, to health challenges or financial disasters, and now a global pandemic. We face obstacles that could become full stops, burying us, making victims of us. They are defining moments that present us with choices. I want to share a framework that has helped me, and could help you, to become more resilient and empowered in the face of any future disruption.

The night of my husband's funeral we held a wake for nearest and dearest friends and family. At around 10 p.m. everyone started to leave, and I started to cry. The reality of my situation hit me with brute force: that nothing would ever be the same again and I had no clue what the future looked like, not even the next day.

A friend, who also happened to be a psychologist, was standing next to me. She said, 'Niks, what's going on for you?' Through my tears, I told her that everything felt like a full stop; it felt like the end of everything I knew. All hopes, dreams and plans shattered. No future.

For someone like me, who is a visionary and likes to have plans not only for next week but for the next couple of years, that was a very scary place to be. I often say that it felt more terrifying than discovering my husband's dead body. Although surreal, that was tangible and there are predictable steps one has to take in the week after someone has died. At this particular moment, at Simon's wake, I was being engulfed in a mist like the one I would experience again later, on the road to Hilton – not knowing what the next step, the next day, let alone my future, would look like.

This friend encouraged me to find my way by seeing the full stop as a comma, as a pause in my life, not the end. She added: 'A comma and dot-dot-dot…, and the dots are the future you are going to create for yourself.'

This thought – a gift my friend gave me in that moment – started to take hold in me in the months that followed, becoming the framework I used to get myself back on my feet and move forward. The ultimate teaching in her analogy was that she charged *me* with taking responsibility for creating *my own* future and not becoming a victim. People walk into our lives to reflect us back at ourselves. They are perfect mirrors in any given moment, helping us discover who we really are and how we want to live.

Over the past three years of discovering what it really means to walk through the shadow of the valley of death – the shadowlands, as I call it – those dots have been made up of new people, new places, new experiences and new possibilities, by choice. My husband's death opened the door to an unexpected journey of personal enquiry, if I was prepared to embrace who Nikki is – Nikki without Simon, with whom I had shared my life for twenty-eight years. Opening my head and heart to new ways of being and doing in the world has been both terrifying and exhilarating at the same time. I stepped through the door, and while going through the mountains and valleys of pain, grief and growth, I experienced a transformation on every level of my being, in both my personal and professional life.

When I think back to other disruptions – the lower-back injury, an expensive business-partnership decision that cost me dearly in peace of mind and money, a ruptured disc in my neck, and starting as a beginner in a brand-new career after two successful careers before that, among other things – all of these presented me with the option of a comma or a full stop. All of these were full of the risks that come with stepping into the unknown, and all of these demanded that I take responsibility for my role in them and my role in stepping through the door and moving forward. Here's the crux, though: no one can do it for you.

When I share the Comma Full Stop© framework with my audiences, I follow up by suggesting: If any of you are holding onto something from your past that you are allowing to keep you prisoner – as a full stop – perhaps in this moment you can see yourself turning that full stop into a comma, allowing yourself to be broken open instead of remaining a victim.

So many people have told me how much this framework has helped them to identify what they have been holding on to and what has been holding them back. One woman said that after attending my talk she cried for eight hours straight. She had not let herself cry for eighteen years, all the while holding on tightly to a traumatic experience. What an incredible release! I have heard many other stories about rebirth and reinvention because of a simple choice at a particular moment.

COMMA OR FULL STOP? YOU CHOOSE!

Whatever has happened to you, whatever you are processing: What was or is it that might be holding you back? Can you find the courage to say that it is not a full stop for you? That it's a comma, and not the end, and that your life will go on? That you will continue to find joy and move towards the light?

There is no better time than now to reframe and re-author your life. Now is the time to take practical steps to give you peace of mind so that you can live life to the full. The only moment you have is *now*!

Take a moment to reflect and note down some standout What If™ moments that have disrupted your life, and whether they are, or have been, a comma or a full stop.

EXERCISE
WHAT IF™ MOMENT

Describe it: ______________________________
____
____

Comma or full stop? ______________________________
____
____

Main lessons it taught you:
____
____
____
____
____

*

WHAT IF™ MOMENT

Describe it: ____
____
____

Comma or full stop? ____
____
____

Main lessons it taught you:
____
____
____
____
____

*

WHAT IF™ MOMENT

Describe it: ____
____
____

Comma or full stop? ____
____
____

Main lessons it taught you:
____
____
____
____
____

*

This exercise may be copied for personal use.

I do believe that no experiences, good or bad, are wasted if we can reframe them. The Comma Full Stop© analogy is a reframing technique that can be extremely helpful to start your transformation through the fire of disruption. Even experiences we wouldn't wish on our worst enemy can be stepping stones towards a deeper, richer life experience. It all depends how you perceive them.

Takeaways for winning at work

- See yourself as an explorer, not a military-style defender who is at war
- Explorers are curious and open to new ways of doing and being in the world
- If a team member is going through a tough time, acknowledge that they are going through a challenging time, but that you believe that with time, help and seeing their way to turning the full stop moment into a comma, they will get through it

Takeaways for winning at home and life

- No matter how traumatic your current situation may be, everything is figureoutable
- The truth is that nothing good or bad lasts forever
- Go and visit those dark places in your heart and mind – really go there, but don't get stuck there
- Take responsibility for your journey

Chapter 11

Let your glitter settle

It's not only major life-altering events that provide us with the opportunity to grow our resilience muscle. 'Glitter storms' are a daily occurrence in all our lives. Things happen that disturb us, stress us, throw us off our game and make us anxious. While we are in the glitter storm, things are messy and unclear, and we feel out of control. The key to surviving it is to give your glitter time to settle. If you let it, it always does.

I picked up the very helpful analogy of the glitter storm from a book called *Under Pressure* by Lisa D'Amour, which confronts the epidemic of stress and anxiety in girls in particular. However, I believe the glitter-storm concept works for us all.

Imagine you have your own glitter jar in front of you (if you have a real one, all the better). Pick it up and give it a good shake for a few seconds to create a glitter storm. This storm represents any issues that are stressing you out or causing anxiety in your life. Look at it: this is what it feels like in your brain and heart right now. Once you have identified the issues that are causing you emotional discomfort while shaking the jar, put it down and watch the glitter slowly float to the bottom. What I like about the jar analogy is that it shows you that you need to give the glitter time and space to settle. Just watching it settle is therapeutic in and of itself. It's a practical exercise in mindfulness.

When you are upset, supercharged emotions can hijack your whole neurological system, putting you in a state of panic or paralysis. Your ability to function optimally is reduced and you lose your perspective: everything is terrible or just too much. You become a victim of your own fears and wild thinking, spinning in a cyclone of distress. You start to feed your anxiety by overreacting.

When we feel out of control, we instinctively want to go into over-control mode to take back our power. This is very often counter-productive. We need to first slow down and take a few minutes to let our glitter settle, be a little patient with ourselves, wonder aloud, take a walk, sleep on it or even colour in a picture or build part of a puzzle. In other words, we need to take a step back and breathe.

D'Amour says that anxiety and stress are forms of emotional discomfort that act as warning signs for us to take constructive action or to stop doing something that doesn't serve us or is dangerous to us. But emotional discomfort is not always a bad thing. The trick is not to ignore the glitter storm but to sidestep the melodrama before it becomes all-consuming and destructive. Here are some steps you can take:

- Acknowledge that what you are experiencing (or the situation you are in) is horrible and less than desirable (in fact, it stinks, says D'Amour)
- Also acknowledge that it can be handled (there is a solution for most things)
- Slow down and allow your glitter to settle
- Give yourself the gift of a little time and space (even ten minutes can make a difference, enabling you to diffuse your anxiety and distress and deal with things more effectively)
- Once you have identified the sources of your stress and anxiety, play the game of 'worst-case scenario' (catastrophise by asking yourself what the worst thing is that could happen and what the consequences of that might be; often your situation turns out to be not quite as bad as you thought)
- Now you can reframe the issues as 'on your way, not in your way' because you have perspective and can implement solutions
- Follow up this reframing with a plan of action to change or diffuse the issues that you *can* control.

These steps provide a simple exercise that will help you develop coping skills to build resilience. Every time you overcome a glitter storm, you build your confidence a little more. You get 'glitter-storm fit', developing an inner knowledge that you've got this. You discover that while you can't control the world around you, you *can* control your reaction to it. You have the power to re-author situations and circumstances by choosing your own response to them. This is within your power. Every time.

A snow globe or glitter jar is a powerful visual metaphor that illustrates that mindfulness – the cultivation of stillness in the face of the swirling chaos of life – is hugely important. It helps us see that we need to choose not to get caught up permanently in a glitter storm and become victims of circumstance. Instead, we must choose to empower ourselves and each other by first letting our glitter settle and then reframing and re-authoring our response to the storm. Take a breath, or two or three. Shake that glitter jar. Whether at work or at home, you've got this!

Takeaways for winning at work

- You will not always be able to manage your colleagues, your boss, your suppliers, or the micro- or macroeconomic environment, but you can manage your own responses to challenges
- Acknowledge all the aspects that are contributing to your storm: don't ignore them, as this will allow your inner wounds to fester
- Remember that one drowning person cannot save another, so find support to help you deal with your own stress and anxiety
- People feel safe with you when they believe you can keep perspective. Learning to reframe an experience is a fantastic skill, particularly for leaders or aspiring leaders, as you can then help others do the same for themselves
- Help mentor others in your circle who are 'losing it' by teaching them the glitter-storm concept – it can help enormously to talk things through with someone else
- Remember that most of us have the answers to our problems within ourselves, but sometimes we need another person there so that we can get an issue out of our head, or to stop us from going around in circles and creating more anxiety

Takeaways for winning at home and life

- Families are made up of human beings who are unpredictable because they are emotional and multisensory – unlike robots
- Your children and your partner will have glitter storms (and so will you)
- If you can accept that glitter storms will come and go, and that they are part of learning how to deal with life with confidence, you can invite them in as a teacher for every member of your family. Acceptance will strengthen your belief that you will get through them and build resilience at the same time
- Teach your family how to deal with glitter storms and how to let their glitter settle
- Make a family glitter jar – or a glitter jar for each family member
- At the end of every week, acknowledge and celebrate all the glitter storms you have faced as individuals or a family, and what they have taught you; this is a great way to keep stress and anxiety in perspective in family life – and what a valuable life skill to give your kids and yourself!
- As a parent, you need to take responsibility for your own stress and anxiety, because parental anxiety is the most infectious thing in the world. Your children can read even the most subtle cues in your face or demeanour. This will fuel their fears. By dealing with your own issues, you will make them feel safer and empower them to reframe their anxiety and bring down their own stress levels because they see you doing it for yourself

Chapter 12

Learning to balance pressure and tension

Do you remember learning how to drive a manual car and getting stuck in first gear? That is what unchecked stress feels like. In the same way that we learn how to shift gears up and down in a car, we need to get the balance between pressure and tension right.

When we stay in distress for too long, anxiety and eventually burnout can result. In fact, 60 per cent of visits to doctors today are stress-related. In 2019 the World Health Organization made workplace burnout an official diagnosis. Those who have experienced it know that it often takes at least six months to a year to recover from burnout caused by extreme mental and physical exhaustion.

However, in our concern about too much stress, we should not lose sight of the fact that there needs to be sufficient tension and pressure within a system, and in ourselves, to ensure that we can be effective. We need to be able to perform – not over-perform – on a daily basis at work, in a learning environment at any age (for example, when studying for a test or an exam), or when preparing for a big presentation.

Getting the balance between tension and pressure right means we will move between eustress (positive stress) and distress (negative stress). We need to understand that stress is not only negative; it can have an upside too. We need enough stress to win at both life and work. But we need to be tuned in to its nuances.

Often, high achievers are the ones who end up burning out. We are seeing this in high school, at universities and in the workplace. High achievers can get stuck in the cycle of overachieving. We are also seeing it in families who experience conflict and extreme, constant stress. In my 'Children Living in the Red Zone' talk for parents,[23] I use the analogy of a pressure gauge. I talk about the fact that there is rarely a child moving into the high-pressure zone whose parents aren't also in the red zone in some way. We often tend to mirror each other's stress. And we need to acknowledge that we are seeing extreme overwork in the pandemic work-from-home scenario, with employees trying to prove they are working hard and that they deserve to keep their jobs even though no one can 'see' them in the virtual working world.

NEGATIVE STRESS WEARS US DOWN

Prior to Covid-19, I was noticing more and more children stuck in fight-or-flight mode – that stuck-in-first-gear feeling when driving a manual car. It's an extremely uncomfortable state to be in. You can feel the strain on the vehicle, and you can hear it too. Fight-or-flight mode is the result of constant stress triggers. Adults experience this too, but because we have more life experience, we *should* have greater self-awareness to make sense of our stress and manage it before it gets out of control. Everyone's stress threshold is slightly different, though, and we must bear this in mind. Some people can take more stress than others.

TOO LITTLE STRESS IS NOT GOOD FOR US EITHER

A great example of how students need pressure and tension to perform is that of learners writing matric exams – especially those who have been high performers in extracurricular activities, ranging from sports to performing arts. These young people would have been training and practising hard, long hours, with discipline and under supervision, often for six out of seven days a week. Then, a month or two before prelims, it all stops. The pressure and structure these young people have been used to falls away, including:

- Exercise routines – often externally imposed
- Race or match schedules
- Fitting their studies into tight time allocations
- Being hyper-focused when they do study, because they won't have another chance
- Eating well to support the physical demands of their regime
- Having a coach on hand all the time to ensure they are up to speed and to encourage them to stay the course

- Being part of a team, meaning they are supported and encouraged by each other and they perform for each other
- A regular flood of endorphins (the happiness hormones that come with exercise and make them feel good)
- Being directed by their own personal goals for achievement
- Being committed to their own success.

They are used to a fair deal of pressure on their systems, and these kids usually do quite well – until they stop exercising, practising and performing and have too much time on their hands. At this point, they can become like an elastic band that has become too loose or has snapped. The same is true for adult extreme athletes – runners, swimmers, cyclists, and iron men and women – and for people who work long hours. When you complete a big, deadline-driven project at work, or have been focused on a competition or race for a few months, don't you often feel flat right after – the next time you exercise, or sit down at your desk? Apart from having felt tired, you'll likely have experienced that the pressure and tension that commanded the performance dissipated, making it difficult to get going again.

CREATING ENOUGH PRESSURE TO PERFORM

I recently counselled a matriculant who fitted this pressure profile. She had returned from representing her country internationally as part of a high-performing sports team that had trained for a year to qualify. She had four weeks to study for prelims. She squandered them, wasting time and wafting around. Her marks in maths and science plummeted by 20 per cent, giving her and her parents a near heart attack, as she was no longer achieving the marks she would need to get into her university course of choice. With matric finals on the horizon, this was hardly the time to not be able to focus and perform.

As I coached her, it became clear that she didn't have enough tension in her system to perform academically. I gave her a loose elastic band to play with. The first thing she did instinctively was to double it over so that she had sufficient tension to push against. She had discovered that it is only interesting to play with an elastic band if there is enough tension for us to get some feedback though our muscles and joints. Without the resistance and pressure, there was nothing to hold her attention, to make her put in effort and work.

It's a great analogy for life – without some kinds of tension or pressure, we can become apathetic. In South African parlance, we become a little 'pap' or 'useless' because we have let go too much. I explained to her that I call this Popped Elastic Band Syndrome, and it's important that we are aware of it. While we need time for recovery from high performance, too much of nothing and no stress is not a good thing. She had lost focus and drive.

It is wise to avoid letting go too much. Popped Elastic Band Syndrome can leave you with insufficient energy, little drive and low work efficiency, all of which will affect your performance at work and at home. Self-awareness, feedback and support from mentors are essential to finding our way to fine-tuning our stress and our need for just enough pressure and tension for effective performance. This is an essential part of emotional intelligence and resilience.

Knowing how much pressure we need and how to create it in a healthy way is a good life skill to develop, for adults and children, but it is often something we avoid because of our fear of stress.

Managing our *distress* is an important part of self-care, but so is ensuring that we have enough *eustress* in our system to perform. Without enough stress, tension and pressure, we become underwhelmed and can feel as demotivated as someone who is in distress. It's a very fine line, isn't it? When there is no stress, time management goes out of the window. Our marks can drop, as can our productivity at work, and we become less self-directed and less motivated to achieve our goals.

ALIGNING THE ELEMENTS OF SUCCESS

We actually need three basic elements to succeed at anything:

- skills to be able to do the task at hand
- the right work rate to get the task done in the allotted time (this is where finding your sweet spot with pressure and tension becomes important)
- a winning attitude to be able to handle a task, galvanise those around you and push beyond the obstacles that may arise.

I run workshops using the licensed Success Cube™ concept to help teams and individuals of all ages write their own Success Recipes for whatever Success Journey they may be on. These recipes are unique to the individual or team, based on discovering their own 'why' behind a Success Journey of any kind. The starting point in this journey of discovery is often very different from the end point, as a team within a leading financial institution I worked with discovered. They started with a focus on creating a Success Recipe for service delivery excellence. In the process they discovered that they could not achieve that while they thought of themselves as the backroom of the organisation (a perception they had no idea they held about themselves until we did some process work). Their breakthrough came when they shifted their own perception from being the backroom to being the backbone of the institution. This change in perception changed everything for them, and service delivery excellence through improved skills, work rate and attitude was then within their reach. They could see it, touch it and understand it.

The beauty of the Success Cube™ concept is that it is a visual, tangible, three-dimensional tool that shows participants where they are now with their skills, work rate and attitude, and where they need to be for the journey and effort to be meaningful to them. The comparison between the two brings a healthy sense of focused pressure and tension in the right places. It's quite remarkable to watch the transformation. To be able to win at work and life, it is necessary for us to find meaning in what we do as a team and as individuals within that team.

Back to my matriculant: once she understood that she needed to create enough pressure and tension in her own system to be able to perform in her final matric exams, I took her through a Success Cube™ process, which showed her where she was currently with her skills, work rate and attitude, and where she needed to be. We created a plan based on that feedback to structure her days with study sessions, completing past papers and exercise. She even took on coaching rhythmic gymnastics in that six-week period to add pressure, expectation, structure and accountability to her days. She put a perfect Success Cube on her desk and, next to it, the structure of the cube in her underperforming state as a reminder of the journey she needed to take to reach her goal. In short, she took control of her attitude, increased her work rate in a meaningful way to her, and knew exactly which skills she needed to sharpen. Her maths and science marks went back up by 20 per cent in the final examinations. She is now studying for the degree she had aimed for and learnt an important life lesson in the process. So: beware of Popped

Elastic Band Syndrome; find that sweet spot between pressure and tension that works *for you.*

Intrinsic motivation is the primary goal, especially with the shift to self-leadership, as we depend less on organisations for validation and affirmation and take more responsibility for winning at work and life. You need to find meaning in your Success Journey for you, even when you are part of a team. Taking responsibility for your own success is an important part of future-proofing yourself through self-leadership.

Understanding the difference between positive and negative stress and how each feels different on our systems is imperative for us to get the balance right. We should always be in a state of dynamic balance: there is no perfect state of static balance.

Stress, tension and pressure are a moving target because we are human beings with a head, a heart and an incredible body that releases chemicals and hormones in response to both internal and external stress. We should be committed to our own self-care. This self-care is not a luxury but a necessity, to avoid getting stuck in a cycle of either overachieving, which can lead to burnout because our battery is totally flat and we have no more resources to recharge it, or under-achieving because we are suffering from Popped Elastic Band Syndrome.

Takeaways for winning at work

- Acknowledge that everyone on your team has different stress thresholds
- Be aware of the stresses on team members both at work and at home; understand that these can change from time to time
- Understand that workplace burnout is a real condition that is often accompanied, among other symptoms, by:
  - emotional and physical exhaustion
  - emotional detachment
  - reduced personal accomplishment
- Help your team members understand that no stress can be as bad as too much stress
- Encourage your team members to find someone who will hold

them accountable and vice versa; this can be extremely helpful, as it creates a supportive relationship: someone to talk to and who can provide feedback
- Help team members identify what creates meaning for them, why it's important to be part of their team, and what nourishment they need to flourish
- Allow for regular reassessment of priorities – ascertain where you or your team are directing your time and energy and whether it is producing the desired results

Takeaways for winning at home and life

- Everyone in the family will have different stress thresholds; for example, one of my children was fine with sport three days a week and the other needed to play sport five days a week to have sufficient dynamic tension in his system
- Everyone needs a bit of tension and pressure to perform optimally
- Teach your family members how to read their own stress response – how much is too much and how much is too little?
- Teach them the difference between positive stress and negative stress
- Teach them to value feedback, because sometimes we can't actually see the full effect of our stress
- Do the Popped Elastic Band exercise with them to illustrate the need for dynamic tension in the system
- Help members of your family work out how much dynamic tension they actually need and, if they do not have enough, how to create more so that they can perform optimally

Chapter 13

Seven steps to regaining a sense of control

Even resilient people need a bit of a kick-start to get going either at the beginning of a new year or after taking a break of any kind (such as a short holiday), especially when things are feeling out of control or when they are going through change. Bringing back routine and structure can do wonders, providing us with boundaries and predictability that make us feel more secure. It's a bit like putting up the side rails of a hospital bed – the patient can't fall out – and it will allay our fear of experiencing some of these feelings that we all have from time to time:

- I'm feeling a bit strange about what lies ahead
- I'm feeling unsettled
- I don't feel confident
- I'm having a bit of a wobble
- I'm not sure what the future holds, so I'm feeling uncertain
- I don't feel prepared for what's coming
- I'm feeling incompetent
- I'm terrified because I've been told everything is changing.

While boundaries and routine help us feel safer and more in control, our brains also need novelty to keep progressing and to feel both inspired and hopeful about the future.

Here are seven steps to help you regain a sense of hope and control in times of uncertainty.

STEP 1: GET BACK INTO ROUTINE

When you take a break, you get out of the normal routine that helps you hold things together on a daily basis. It's important to give yourself the opportunity to change routine from time to time to allow you to recover from the rigours of normal daily life. However, going back into a regular routine is essential to send your brain a signal that it's back to business. You will be amazed at how this will help you regain confidence. It's like getting back in the saddle on a horse or getting back on a bicycle. You return to using well-worn neurological pathways that are familiar, and a sense of comfort and confidence will return. To get back into routine:

- Set a regular wake-up time and bedtime
- Keep regular mealtimes
- Decide what signal you will send to your brain to indicate that the day is done
- Get enough sleep.

STEP 2: START EXERCISING AGAIN

Really keen, competitive sportspeople continue their exercise regimen religiously, whether they are on holiday or not. I'm reasonably regular with my exercise schedule unless I am away or without a regular exercise partner to motivate me. Part of keeping myself fit and healthy, in body and mind, is to include regular exercise in my weekly routine, even if that means committing only to a forty-five-minute walk three times a week and a couple of short sessions of vigorous exercise in between (whatever vigorous means to you – for me that means doing steps or running on the spot). Some benefits of regular exercise include:

- Committing to a regular habit, which gives you a sense of purpose
- Maintaining discipline and a sense of control
- Greasing your joints and your system, which will often get rid of niggles of discomfort or pain without you having to visit a therapist (in my case that would be a physiotherapist or chiropractor)
- Oxygenation of your system for physical healing and oxygen to the brain to keep it sharp
- Pumping endorphins (the happiness hormone) into your system (we could all do with more of that)
- Being screen-free, giving your visual system a break
- Engaging all your senses – more so than if you were looking at a screen

- Building space into your day for yourself – a time when you don't have to respond to any other demands: emails, children, employees, or your boss
- Not multitasking, which is calming
- Letting your mind wander.

STEP 3: TAKE CONTROL OF WHAT YOU EAT

When we are out of our routine or on holiday, we tend to fall off the wagon, eating at strange times and eating what isn't good for us on a regular basis: more alcohol, more sugar and salt, more rich food and more food in general. That's fine when you can have an afternoon siesta to sleep off your excesses, but not when you are having to engage your brain at work and maximise the use of your energy for a minimum of eight hours a day. Some basic guidelines I follow are:

- Reducing my portion size
- Making sure I eat regularly
- Eating more fresh food with lots of fibre
- Drinking lots of water to flush my system of toxins
- Adding a probiotic daily to help rebalance my gut (did you know that 80 per cent of your serotonin comes from your gut?).

STEP 4: INSPIRE YOURSELF

Be aware that your brain needs novelty and newness as well as routine and certainty. Here are some practical ideas for both:

- Clear out your desk – every little last drawer and folder
    - Clutter is dead energy
    - Only keep what is necessary for you to do your job properly, now and in the future
    - Only keep what sparks feelings of joy
    - This activity will tick the box for both novelty and control, creating order out of chaos
- Read *Joy at Work* by Marie Kondo (famous for the KonMari Method) and Scott Sonenshein, about tidying up your physical workspace, digital space, your decisions, your network, your meetings and your team, and restoring order to your job, career and life
- Buy one new thing to liven up your desk – you spend many hours in this spot

    - A new pot plant
    - A new pencil holder
    - Something that is a symbol of a fresh start
- New beginnings can be made at any time in the calendar year
    - Remember: nobody can go back and start a new beginning, but anyone can start today and make a new ending
- Rearrange the furniture in your office or home
    - It switches the energy
    - It moves the eye differently
    - It feels as though you've waved a magic wand
    - It's fun! I do this often in my home and my office
- What is your word for the year?
    - Pick a word that will be your guiding light in all your actions and the decisions you make for the rest of the year
    - One word is also a form of novelty for the brain – a proverbial hook to hang your hat on
    - My word for this year is *transformation.* Last year it was *joy.* What's your word? Whatever you choose, that word will challenge you in the year ahead so that you really understand the meaning of it
    - Read *One Word That Will Change Your Life* by Dan Britton, Jimmy Page and Jon Gordon for the full inside track if you have the time
- Create your vision for the year ahead. I created a PowerPoint presentation in three sections, each with a title that my brain loves and will happily engage with:
    - Joy
    - Growth
    - Excellence
- The brain loves novelty and colour; the beauty of PowerPoint is that you can insert great visuals (find the link to download my Reflections and Vision template in the Other Resources list at the back of this book)
    - Pick one of your chosen visuals to use as a screensaver on your various devices to inspire you often
    - You could also create a vision board for yourself and keep it somewhere where you can see it every day. It will give your brain direction, filling it with positive expectations instead of allowing the psyche to do what it so naturally defaults to (usually thinking negatively)

- Make a list of people who inspire you and make sure you have a quality conversation with at least one of them each week to fill your cup.

STEP 5: MAKE YOURSELF SUPPORTABLE

Human beings are strange creatures. When change throws us a curveball and we feel uncertain, we tend to withdraw. This is partly to take stock and partly because we are embarrassed, fearful or don't want to publicly admit that we might feel out of control and uncertain. Withdrawing and being alone is a very necessary part of dealing with and processing disruption, but don't stay alone for too long, or you might land up in a deep, dark hole. I suggest:

- Creating a mastermind group (so easy to do in the virtual world!)
    - This is a group of similar or diverse people who are all having to adapt to change
    - The group meets regularly (daily, weekly or monthly)
    - It is a great place for brainstorming ideas and then supporting each other with experimentation, accountability and implementation
    - More heads are better than one
- Finding yourself a coach or counsellor
    - Choose someone neutral who can be an objective sounding board for you
- Don't be a victim
    - Don't look for others to name, blame or shame
    - Decide how you can effect change in your life
    - Take responsibility for your choices, attitude and actions
- Keeping perspective
    - What collateral damage and collateral beauty are you experiencing in the situation you find yourself in?
    - Opportunities and possibilities abound if you can get out of a state of being frozen by fear
    - Do my Collateral-Damage vs Collateral-Beauty exercise on page 47.

STEP 6: THINK DIFFERENTLY

The 2020s provide an invitation to think differently about the future – to reimagine life and work as we know it. Rather than doing the same thing quicker, better or more cost-effectively, we need to reimagine what we do.

The same old thinking is not going to get us where we need to go to survive and thrive, today and in the future.

- Challenge yourself to think from the future backwards, even if you can't project too far ahead
  - What do you think the future might look like in one, three or five years' time?
  - How might you have to do your job differently?
  - What do you already have (skills, technology, etc.) that you could implement or use differently?
  - What new skills might you need? Refer to the World Economic Forum's *The Future of Jobs Report* on page 27
  - How can you make better use of the intelligent assistance you already have at your fingertips (e.g. your smartphone); this is a friendly way to look at the benefits of artificial intelligence
  - How are you working with technology differently to deliver more value to your customers or to streamline your own work processes with your team members?
- On a personal front:
  - It's easy to look at your family budget and say, 'We need to cut the spending here and here.' You might succeed by spending less, reducing insurance premiums, or otherwise save a bit of money. But how about looking at changing your behaviour and habits instead?
  - Are you still going to the shops a few times a week for groceries? Why do you do this when you don't have to? Have you thought about what else you could be doing with your time?
  - Consider automating certain kinds of shopping, such as groceries, and making a novelty out of other kinds of shopping. It is a great way to start with something as simple as how you shop. Can you think of intentionally disrupting yourself in this area of your life so that it becomes habitual?

STEP 7: HOLD YOUR FOCUS

With so many challenges surrounding us as we try to find solutions amid external circumstances that are outside our control (think subsequent waves of the coronavirus, a new pandemic and continually changing lockdown restrictions), you may find yourself jumping all over the place. Shiny Object Syndrome is a real thing: we bounce from one good idea or solution to another, never fully immersing ourselves in something or completing anything before moving on. This can lead to high levels of dissatisfaction and demotivation, which can be extremely counter-productive. Here are some tips:

- Look at new ways of doing things
- Look at better ways to use the tools you have at your disposal
- Give all these things some good thought before jumping in:
    - How will it help you on the road to …?
    - How much time will it take?
    - How much money will it earn you?
    - Will it waste your time and energy?
    - How interested are you?
- After some critical analysis, make some clear decisions
    - Narrow down the number of things you are going to work on
    - Decide, truthfully, if it is serving you and/or your organisation, or not
    - If not, stop and do something else
    - To help you with prioritising your time and energy, download my prioritising exercise, which you will find under Other Resources at the end of this book
- Switch off your phone and email alerts at certain times of the day for uninterrupted focus
- Completing a task will give you a degree of satisfaction that raises the level of your happiness hormones and adds to your sense of competence and confidence in your system.

You don't want to be a jack of all trades but master of none, because that would be an unfocused approach that won't give you a sense of growth or progress – which is what you need to raise your satisfaction index. If your effort leads to a sense of satisfaction, even if you land up discarding what you are doing, it is fuel for the fire that will keep you going.

Takeaways for winning at work

When you follow the seven steps to regain a sense of hope and control

- You will give yourself enough predictability to feel more in control and enough novelty and newness to create excitement and hope
- You will have new-found energy and enthusiasm
- You will create more focus and avoid distraction
- You will be coming from a space of exploration, enquiry and curiosity rather than fear
- You will commit to the very necessary journey of reimagining the world of work in the future for yourself
- You will feel a greater sense of control and sanity despite the changes you are facing
- You will generate feelings of progress and satisfaction – even if only small, incremental ones. They all count.
- You will become an example of self-leadership to others
- You will consciously embrace disruption and change rather than be a victim of it

Takeaways for winning at home and life

- Your sense of purpose will make your family feel more grounded
- People will feel safer and will be less reactive because you are calmer
- A regular routine provides family sanity – it's the order of how things happen in the day that counts, regardless of the timing
- Clearing your clutter will enable everyone to follow suit, shifting the energy of your whole home
- You will be an example to the rest of the family by taking responsibility for yourself and showing self-leadership
- Help other family members clarify their purpose and direction for the year
- Consciously embracing disruption as a family by making technology and relationships work for you will result in these positive outcomes:
    - Your children might be able to teach you a thing or two about the functionality of your tech

    - If you are open-minded and invite them to help you, this could revolutionise the way you connect as a family and organise yourselves.
- Remember that togetherness is an important feeling to create in a home, especially when so much is changing and uncertain:
    - What are you creating together?
    - How are you using face-to-face time and technology to connect with each other?

Chapter 14

Grief and loss

Grief (like sex and money) is one of those taboo subjects that no one likes to talk about much. Nevertheless, it is something we will all experience at some point – not only when someone dies, but also when we go through any kind of change, whether positive or negative. Understand that this is empowering, in and of itself. This realisation represents a major 'aha' moment for many of my audience members, and many have thanked me for helping them put words to their feelings.

Let's look at some examples:

- We are going through mass trauma, loss and grief as a result of the coronavirus pandemic – from loss of our autonomy and the way things were to the loss of real people
- When my son's friend, a talented and active sportsperson, had his arm amputated at the age of eighteen because of cancer, he had to mourn the devastating loss of his limb and reframe his experience to continue to thrive. His mother had to do the same
- Boy meets girl, they fall in love, have a white wedding and have children. Many parents have to mourn and let go of this traditional picture when their children announce that they prefer same-sex partners or opt out of marriage and children. The anger and devastation is part of the grieving process, but it's the parents who have the broken picture, not the son or daughter
- Emigration, for all the right reasons, involves a prolonged mourning process that many do not anticipate
- Divorce is the death of what was and the rebirth of something new. Whether the divorce is healthy or acrimonious, it involves adjustment and transition

- Retrenchment forces you to embark on a journey of grief – both for the person being let go and the person doing the retrenching. It is a painful process.

The grieving process is filled with physical, mental and emotional symptoms that are often ignored or brushed aside by the person who is going through the loss and those around them who say, 'Just get over it and move on.' While I am not for a moment encouraging you to hold anyone in a victim space (read Chapter 22 for more on this notion), acknowledging and supporting someone moving through the process is important.

When I share how my husband's death affected my brain and my body, audiences who are now having to cope with the global coronavirus pandemic can identify with me, even though they are going through a different form of loss. Depending on the severity of the loss you have experienced, symptoms can last from a few weeks to months or even years. Regardless of the duration, if you experience this process consciously, you can experience an enormous amount of growth and reinvention.

This is not an exhaustive list, but here are some of the symptoms of shock and grief that I experienced, and which affected my brain and body.

MY BRAIN

- Sudden onset of ADD-like symptoms, causing an inability to concentrate for the first couple of months
- I had the concentration span of a flea for the first year and it took a full two years before I felt like I was able to fully focus again, at will
- With cortisol and adrenalin flooding my system, I was in constant fight-or-flight mode – anything could distract me
    - I lost all interest in reading for pleasure because I couldn't slow down my brain enough to enjoy the process – books were merely words on a page
    - As an avid reader, it was devastating to no longer be able to escape into a book
    - I couldn't sleep and had to resort to sleeping tablets for around eighteen months
- Mild obsessive-compulsive disorder, which developed from a need to control the uncontrollable in the first few weeks

  - Every aspect of my life had completely blown up and been ripped apart
  - I would find myself unpacking and repacking my handbag
  - I was neurotic about having enough toilet paper in the house
- Low brain-processing power, like a computer with low RAM
  - I processed slowly; I connected dots slowly
  - My ears were hearing what my husband's executor was saying, but when she was twenty minutes in, I was still working out what she had said fifteen minutes earlier!
  - Dealing with executors and financial advisors and reading through twenty-page legal documents taxed my brain, and I often needed someone to explain things to me in plain English
  - My brain felt like mush
- Memory loss and poor working memory
  - This aspect was terrifying to me. I would have a great conversation with someone and then not remember a thing about what was said, or I would remember the conversation but not with whom I had had it
  - I would lose my train of thought or forget my words in the middle of a presentation or interview and hit a complete blank
  - As I was aware of this, I could warn my audiences!

When I look at this list it is a miracle that I was able to work at all in the first year of my bereavement. I went back to work two months after my husband's death. I could take that long a break because I was self-employed, and also because this happened around Christmas, when business slows down anyway. Spare a thought for people employed full-time, who are usually granted only three days of compassionate leave. Work was good for me, though – it was the one place where I still felt competent and experienced a sense of familiarity when every other part of my life was hell. There was also a measure of predictability.

MY EMOTIONS

- I felt raw and vulnerable, as if my skin had been ripped right off me
- Depression

    - I see-sawed between being really okay and laughing, and bursting into tears within a few minutes of each other
    - I eventually made the decision to take antidepressants and sleeping tablets for about eighteen months, in addition to counselling, coaching and integration work to deal with the trauma
- Irritability about everything and anything – from poor customer service while navigating the bureaucratic nightmare of wrapping up a life to snapping at people because I was so exhausted
- I couldn't fall asleep naturally at night; power naps, which I used be able to take at will during the day, became impossible
- Low resilience and tolerance
- Panic attacks
    - I couldn't breathe
    - I couldn't see
    - I couldn't find my way using a map when I walked around a city overseas, and I couldn't make sense of verbal directions from passers-by who tried to help me – my senses literally shut down and I holed up in a restaurant with tears silently pouring down my cheeks, waiting for a friend to come and rescue me, after which I couldn't get out of bed for two days
- Plenty of crying
    - I had never been an easy crier, so this was actually quite a liberating part of grief for me
    - I truly learnt to let go; who knew a body could hold so many tears?
- Red-hot anger – at my husband for putting himself in harm's way, at our attackers for whom life was cheap, at my country that had let me down, and at poor customer service and incompetence.

MY BODY

For a year I suffered from:

- A constant knot in my stomach and a stomach ache
- Nausea to the point of dry retching when I was building up for a cry, which was often
- Diarrhoea

- Frequent need to urinate
- A very dry mouth
- A metallic taste in my mouth for six months
- Hand tremors that also impacted my ability to write
- Tripping, and falling up and down stairs: in a shock or crisis, the body brings all its energy to the centre for survival, and the extremities are the last to receive any (note how many elderly people fall and break a wrist, ankle or hip after they have lost a spouse)
- Hair loss
- Shingles
- Eczema
- Weight gain: I had always been very slim and weighed fifty-four kilograms when Simon died. Everyone worried that I would fade away, but my body did the opposite and over a year I gained twelve kilograms. I have since lost five kilograms without dieting, but it only dropped off nearly three years on.

If you have a family or are leading a team, it is very important that you make your team members aware of what the grieving process looks like when going through disruption and loss. People need to acknowledge their grief and their feelings. One of the worst things you can do is sweep complex feelings under the carpet. There is huge potential for growth and learning if you are prepared to work with your grief. If you do not deal with grief, it festers inside you and comes out in destructive ways over time that could result in self-sabotage and team sabotage. Find someone to talk to. See a counsellor, coach or psychologist. Do some integration work between your body and emotions. Grief and trauma live on in your body and your cells. Dealing with it intellectually is one thing, but going deeper into your emotional being is quite another. That is where the real growth happens.

For me, processing grief and change is an active process. 'Grieving' is an '-ing' word, a verb, indicating that you are doing something. No amount of reading books about grief can be a proper substitute for 'doing' grief.

PROCESSING GRIEF

People continue to process the changes that come with any kind of loss in some shape or form. However, you do not have to remain a victim! I *did* grief for the first two years by:

- crying
- talking
- sleeping
- walking
- swimming
- journaling
- praying
- meditating
- reflecting
- growing
- changing
- absorbing
- accepting
- healing
- discovering.

Importantly, this process of recovery has become an adventure of rediscovering myself – almost a rebirth. I believe it would have been an oversight to omit this perspective on grief. I included it in the book because it forms part of the context for this conversation on disruption. It adds another layer of complexity and interference that individuals, parents, business people, team leaders and management have to take into consideration and work through. There is always an upside when grief and trauma are handled well: it manifests in growth, learning and resilience.

Working with disruption requires courage, open-mindedness, and a desire to see windows and doors open when looking through the right lens. If you think the whole world is against you, it will be difficult to see the positives. Attitude is key.

Takeaways for winning at work

- Be aware that work is important for recovery but may also distract you from dealing with your new reality of loss
- Make sure a team member who is going through grief has a support structure – someone to talk to, counselling, and so on
- You may need to allow extra time off for the person to deal with practical changes in their lives, such as wrapping up an estate, finding childcare, and so on
- Refer to Chapter 4 for insights into the seven stages of adjustment and transition – it will help you and the team member to understand where they are in the process

Takeaways for winning at home and life

- It is not only your mind that will be affected by the grief process, but your body and emotions too
- Grief is not linear and you will circle back to previous stages over and over
- Grief is a process that takes time, and you need to allow for this without keeping the family member in a victim space – support, but don't rescue
- Motion shifts emotion – get up off the couch and move – it will help!
- You will need time with people for support and to talk, but you will also need time alone to process what you are going through
- Grief is situational: how someone is able to deal with it will differ from person to person and depend on circumstances. A person left with young children to care for will not have as much time as I have had to focus on their recovery process (my children were eighteen and twenty-two at the time). We need to keep in mind that no two situations are identical
- Do not compare your grief with someone else's – what you are going through right now is big for you
- One person's experience is not more profound than someone else's
- Remember that no matter how bad this may feel, it too shall pass – it's little solace, but I can tell you that it is true

Chapter 15

The importance of stopping

Wisdom can be found in the most unplanned moments and unexpected places. This is what happened to me one day when I was feeling frenzied and frazzled before 9 a.m. As an antidote to the stress I was experiencing because of having way too much to do and not enough time in which to do it, I decided to go for a brisk walk to de-stress. That is what most of the gurus and books tell you, right? Exercise will do the trick.

I put on my running shoes and my smartwatch and set off at a pace to walk my sillies out. But I found the walk had the opposite effect. The more I walked, the more I stressed. I couldn't breathe, my heart was racing, and I was most certainly not calming down. This is not how I was supposed to be feeling. I wanted to feel better, not worse! I needed to clear my head, not feel like it was full of fluffy cotton wool. I needed clarity, not feelings of overwhelm. How was I going to cope with the rest of my day, which was already crowding in on me, making it hard to breathe and concentrate?

So I stopped and did something completely counter-intuitive: I found a resting place. It was at a bird hide on the other end of the park in the estate where I lived, and it overlooked a little dam. I climbed the wooden stairs to the thatched viewing deck and sat down, surveying the scene in front of me, watching flocks of little birds swooping and soaring, and listening to their melodious chatter. Then I saw, right in the middle of the lake on the island, a mother blue crane sitting on her nest of eggs. She just sat there, placid but determined. Patiently. Peacefully. Seemingly doing nothing.

And so I just sat, staring at her – breathing in her presence, her peace and acceptance. She was not rushing around. She was not multitasking like us bizarre human beings. She was just sitting, doing the most important job in the world: incubating her eggs. At some point I got up and did some slow, long stretches with deep inhales and exhales, bringing me back into my body, all the while maintaining eye contact with 'my' crane. After I had communed with her for half an hour, I was feeling much more grounded. I reluctantly descended the stairs and took a slow walk back home, to reality.

I proceeded to have the most wonderful day because I had shifted my perspective. Nothing was as urgent as I had thought. I had brought myself out of my panic and had managed to bring down my pressure out of the red zone. I was engaging with life again from the perspective of love, not fear, and it made all the difference.

Over the weeks that followed, whenever I felt the need to recalibrate and rebalance myself, I took my soul for a walk to see 'my' mother crane. She taught me the meaning of slowing down and smelling the roses, that not everything is so urgent that it has to be done right now, and that *I* need to sometimes ask whether I am being kind to myself.

When mental confusion and overwhelm engulf me, it is a warning: time to sit up, take note, create space between myself and the frenzy out there, and decide what it is that I need. What I don't need to do is more stuff. I usually need to stop and simply *be* for a while.

I've learnt that it's okay to say to myself, 'Not now. Slow down and listen. Listen for that voice inside that knows exactly what you need and where you need to be. Slow down enough to "feel" that voice and to trust that it is there to help you instead of covering up the out-of-control feeling that comes with doing more.' Does this sound familiar? There is a wise soul inside each of us that knows just what we need. Listen and learn. Find yourself a blue crane.

Takeaways for winning at work

- In results-oriented environments we constantly go, go, go – when stopping might be just what we need to do to improve our performance
- Self-reflection reminds us of who we are and what is important; this often gets lost in the rush and pressure
- When last did you really stop and simply sit?

Takeaways for winning at home and life

- You need to claim some 'me time' to be a better parent, with no one asking you for help, and without doing anything, even if it is only for fifteen minutes a day
- If you can organise for someone to look after your children while you take your 'me time', you will relax into it even more
- Monitor your personal pressure gauge and take remedial action before you lose control
- Remember: you make your worst parenting decisions when you are stressed
- Practise the 4:7:8 breathing method to calm down (in for a count of four, hold for seven counts, then breathe out slowly for eight counts). Doing this a few times will calm and slow you down so that you can get in touch with yourself. You can then ask yourself, calmly:
    - What does my head say?
    - What does my heart say?
    - What does my gut tell me?

Chapter 16

Disruption is like a Mystery Box Challenge

Future-proofing yourself to win at work and life is both an attitude and a broad set of skills and behaviours. More than anything, it is about accepting that change is going to happen, that we have to learn how to deal with it, and get comfortable with the unexpected. Disruption is like a *Masterchef* Mystery Box Challenge. In fact, life is a series of disruptions of all kinds – ranging from adopting new technologies to relationship make-ups and break-ups, to new schools and jobs, to a global pandemic and working from home, to death or disease, and so much more.

I am always fascinated how each *Masterchef* competitor comes up with unique solutions (dishes) when given the same mystery box of ingredients, none of which are of their own choosing. Sometimes contestants like what they get and sometimes they don't. Sometimes they have never cooked with some of the ingredients in the box. Regardless, they embrace the creative challenge, problem-solving with what they have. Interestingly, they often do better with a limited ingredient selection and a narrow brief than when they are given free run of the pantry to make anything they like.

While *Masterchef* is a cooking competition, I think the personal development that contestants experience, and the resilience they develop while learning and doing something under pressure, is quite extraordinary. Imagine if we reframed our challenging experiences as Mystery Box Challenges instead of problems? It is what it is, and everything is figureoutable. Everything you go through – all the positive and negative experiences – can help you be better than or more than you were yesterday. They add richness to your repertoire of how you do life and how you accommodate and adapt to change.

There are two vital questions we should be asking ourselves every time we face disruption:

- What can we learn from this?
- How can we grow from this?

The answers make the discomfort worthwhile. They represent the self-reflection work that is necessary to keep us moving forward. At the end of the day, fear of change as a source of energy is not sustainable, but curiosity is. How curious are you?

Words have power. Reframing a disruptive moment as a Mystery Box Challenge could open the door to a completely new way of thinking that may yield some interesting results. Try it. You may surprise yourself and your team at home or at work.

Takeaways for winning at work

- When you have your next team meeting to discuss tackling a new challenge, frame it as a Mystery Box Challenge
    - Identify the challenge: What has to change?
    - Identify the ingredients
    - Divide the team into groups so that a variety of different solutions are generated
- You may want to do a team-building Mystery Box Challenge that involves a real cook-off in a test kitchen prior to having to tackle a big disruption conversation so that everyone starts thinking outside the box
- Do group reflection work using these two questions:
    - What did we learn from this?
    - How did we grow from this?

Takeaways for winning at home and life

- I find some of the most interesting meals are the ones that have to be created out of nothing, so don't go shopping – rather use the limited ingredients you have in the pantry and fridge

  - This is an exercise in resourcefulness and thinking outside the box
  - It's also a good way to save money and reduce food wastage
- Get your kids into the kitchen and involve them in cooking and baking
  - It's science in action, as ingredients change state
  - Even if the dish is a disaster, they get to see how you can disrupt a recipe by changing an ingredient or even over-salting a dish
- When children face a tough new experience, such as going to a new school or having to break into a new friendship circle
  - Affirm that while they may be uncomfortable, you know they can do this
  - Help them identify what they are learning from the experience and how they are growing from it
  - Self-awareness can never start too young: age eight is a good time to start
- With teens you can do cook-offs (parents versus teens, or one teen and one parent versus the other teen and parent)
  - There is nothing like a bit of friendly competition
  - Create new memories that you can happily recall in the years to come: 'Remember when ...'

Chapter 17

Getting yourself out of a funk

If you find yourself getting into a funk or are feeling a bit low, lost and as if you are losing focus, don't wait too long to take yourself in hand. Whether your feelings are the result of normal daily stress or the global pandemic, here are some practical strategies that I have used to 'pull myself out of it' that may just help you too.

RE-EVALUATE HOW YOU ARE MAKING DECISIONS

Sometimes we get into a rut, doing things for the sake of it without questioning our level of interest or passion, or the financial viability and time investment. If what you are doing is not giving you enough reward, ditch it. Here is a simple re-evaluation exercise:

- Create a table with five columns
- List the items you are busy with in the left-hand column
- Label the other columns: income, time, interest and passion
- Give yourself a score out of 10 in the interest and passion columns
- Record the amount of money the activity will generate for you in the income column
- Record the time an activity takes in the time column.

Table 2: Prioritising sheet

PRIORITISING FOR: ______________________________

ITEM	INCOME	TIME	INTEREST	PASSION
	R		/10	/10

You may be very surprised at the result (I certainly was). It shows clearly what serves you and what doesn't, and you will stop doing certain things immediately. You can find the template download link under Other Resources at the back of this book.

SEE YOURSELF THROUGH A NEW LENS

I came across Marcus Buckingham's work many years ago. One of his hallmarks is that he encourages people to focus on their strengths instead of spending time trying to improve on their weaknesses. His book, *Find Your Strongest Life*, was a landmark read in my professional development. During the pandemic he has been offering his online StandOut® Strengths Assessment free of charge (but if you have to pay for it, do it anyway!) to affirm what the greatest gifts are that you bring to a team, in a quick and interesting way that takes only twenty minutes.[24] This is a great activity to do for yourself, and a fabulous one to do as a team. I have used this assessment with small and large teams with great success. It really helps individuals see and appreciate themselves, and it helps teams see how diverse their strengths are and who has which strengths. Buckingham's list includes: creator, teacher, connector, influencer, pioneer, advisor, provider, stimulator, equalizer. The assessment shows your top two strengths. For example, I am a creator–teacher. The seventeen-page report you receive is full of insights and accurate nuggets of information about you that will truly help you see yourself through a different lens, appreciate your team members more, and match tasks more appropriately to people.

MANAGE YOUR INNER CRITIC

Yes, we all have an inner critic: that little voice inside us that creates Imposter Syndrome and makes us feel inadequate. I am a fan of Julia Cameron's tool from her wildly successful book *The Artist's Way*, called Morning Pages: every morning, Cameron advises, get up and write whatever comes to mind, without judgement – whether this is a whinge, whine, complaint, boast about yourself to yourself, or involves questioning yourself or filling line after line with the words 'I don't know what to write'. I find it amazing how much clarity we have when we get things out of our heads and onto a page. You can destroy the pages afterwards; no need to keep them to reread later. The idea is to create a regular habit that releases and uncovers more than you could ever imagine in the process. We don't know what is getting in our way of success or healing, but our Morning Pages can be very revealing.

GET MOVING IN NATURE

Move beyond your computer screen and the four walls of your office. Be a tourist in your own town. Some of the things that helped me reboot have included walking through local parks and botanical gardens, hiking a wilderness trail through a game reserve and gardening. Access to wide open spaces feeds our visual system with new images, which are important for creative thinking and problem-solving. The exercise, sunshine and fresh air will always do you good. Psychologists say that motion shifts emotion, which is probably why swimming, while I was in the depths of processing my grief, was so important to me. Getting away from everyone and everything, being immersed in water and doing a form of moving meditation by swimming length after length was important for my entire being. We have to create moments when we can get out of our heads and away from having to perform and deliver.

TRY SOMETHING NEW

Bored of doing the same things over and over? Do something new. It's refreshing! Tired of eating the same old things over and over? Try a new recipe! It wakes up your taste buds! Tired of watching the same types of movies or series? Watch movies and TV series you wouldn't normally watch. It's stimulating! All you need to do is look at someone else's profile on a streaming service like Netflix to see how the algorithm keeps offering you more of the same. Try something off someone else's list – you might enjoy it. Take yourself off to an art gallery – you may love it or hate it, and either is okay.

TIDY AND CHUCK OUT YOUR STUFF

Clear out cupboards and drawers. Give away what you don't need and then reorganise what you keep when you pack it away. If it is not useful or doesn't give you a sense of joy, get rid of it. I know this is rich coming from me, as I tend to be a hoarder, but I have been doing a fair amount of chucking, clearing, giving away and reorganising lately, and it feels so good!

GROW SOMETHING

Many people who had lived with a beautiful garden for years said that during lockdown they were seeing and appreciating their garden as if for the first time. Plant a patch of new plants in your garden. Move existing plants around. I love every season in my garden. New growth in spring brings new hope; autumn is a signal of huge change; and winter is for hibernation and changing pace. And if you don't have a garden, go and buy yourself some new pot plants.

GO WITHOUT A LIST FOR A DAY

Yes, this is ironic coming from me, the list queen, but I try to use lists as seldom as possible on weekends. It's a way of taking my hands off life's steering wheel and giving up control for a while. Give it a go! It will feel strange at first, but it is good for you to allow life to unfold a little on its own and do what you are drawn to rather than what you have to do, even if it is only for half a day.

SOCIALISE SAFELY

Socialising with others boosts our energy levels; we are social creatures who are suffering from isolation fatigue at present. Find your own way to socialise safely at this time. Hiking and cycling with friends would be good for many different reasons.

Takeaways for winning at work

- Re-evaluate how you are making decisions by looking at where you are directing your time and attention
- The prioritising exercise in this chapter will help you take the emotion out of making decisions
- Make time to use a new profiling tool to gain a fresh perspective on yourself or your team
- It's important to get away from your screen regularly and do something else for a while
- Silence your inner critic so that you can alleviate Imposter Syndrome at work

- Take action to boost your emotional agility and resilience in multisensory ways that involve movement and the outdoors on a regular basis

Takeaways for winning at home and life

- Multisensory activities are essential
    - They balance out time in front of a screen
    - They shift your emotions and make you a nicer partner and better parent
    - They are important for managing stress
    - They remind you that you are a human *being*, not a human *doing*
    - They provide a holistic form of self-care from the inside out
- If you spend time killing your inner critic, you will be much less critical of others – strangely, we take our own unresolved issues out on others
- We can get very emotional when we have to make decisions in a family situation – use the prioritising exercise to see where you may be wasting your time and money

PART 4

LEADING YOURSELF

Covid-19 is beckoning you to dance with disruption. It is a signal for you to start preparing yourself with intention and purpose for a future that will be filled with the multitude of disruptions I have been alluding to in this book. Over and above developing your internal resilience, I suggest taking action to empower yourself with the right mindset, attitude and skills, remembering that you are always a work in progress. As the world continues to shift and change, so must you in your personal and professional capacities. As Ancient Chinese philosopher Lao Tzu said, 'He who knows others is wise. He who knows himself is enlightened.'

Unless you were already working from home, or working for yourself, working from home signals a distinct shift to self-leadership. Individuals who have been used to being micromanaged in the workplace now find themselves adrift and responsible for their own choices and actions every minute of every day. At the same time, leaders and managers have found themselves feeling somewhat out of control and having to trust that their staff will show up and do what needs to be done – driven by their own internal locus of control. I believe this is a moment in history that will see the human resources playbook being rewritten.

Management guru Tom Peters was already talking about the end of corporate responsibility and the beginning of renewed personal responsibility in 2005. He called it 'an extraordinary opportunity to take charge of our own lives'. I believe that this is even more pertinent today than ever before. Employees have become extremely dependent on their organisations and are not developing the entrepreneurial and self-management skills that would enable them to survive outside an organisation on their own (a distinct possibility for many, as businesses begin outsourcing to cater for on-demand needs instead of employing people full-time) or bring fresh entrepreneurial thinking to a business.

Start treating yourself more as a business. This way, you will transform yourself by building yourself as an asset of constantly increasing value. You do not want to be part of the 85–90 per cent of employees globally who are disengaged at work. A serious Popped Elastic Band Syndrome pandemic is happening in the world of work right now (we already looked at this syndrome on page 106). Lack of personal development and self-awareness goes hand in glove with this. The statistic from the World Economic Forum's *The Future of Jobs Report* of October 2020 noted that only 42 per cent of employees are currently taking up employer-supported reskilling and upskilling opportunities.

We are overdue for this shift to self-leadership. For too long we have seen individuals becoming more and more dependent on external validation, acknowledgement, recognition, leadership and motivation. This dependency on a company or organisation has become a form of disempowerment. The signs have been there for many years as companies have spent increasing amounts of time, energy and money motivating people to simply do their jobs.

Management panic and fear have led to the development of often complex and expensive leadership solutions that miss the mark. We need to change our focus to putting the human – you and me – in the middle of it all. Let's revisit and repackage ourselves so that we are better prepared for disruption of any kind, develop the ability to leverage our Brand of One (more on this concept in Chapter 19), and can create meaningful life experiences in any team in which we participate – at work or in life.

Chapter 18

Define yourself by who you are, not by what you do

How often are we defined by our job title? And yet this is not who we are, but merely what we do. I met a woman at a wedding eight years ago, and we got chatting, as one does. She was employed at one of the large banks, designing financial products. When I enquired what she had studied, she said she was a qualified architect. In fact, she had wanted to study fashion design, but her parents didn't think that was a valid career, which is how she landed up doing architecture. We dug a little deeper because I was fascinated. It turned out that as long as she was designing or building something, she was happy – whether a dress, a building or a financial product.

About four years later I bumped into her and enquired if she was still with the same bank. The answer was that she had moved on – and now had the best job in the world. She had joined a new emerging online bank and was helping to build it from the ground up. Then she added, 'And I'm designing dresses as a side hustle.' She couldn't be happier.

This a classic story of someone who knows her essence and understands her innate talent – what gets her up in the morning, what lights her fire. She truly understands her core strengths and passions and has put them to work for her to create a meaningful life that leads to enormous satisfaction on every level. She is a classic example of someone who is doing something:

- she loves
- she is good at
- the world needs
- the world is prepared to pay her for.

This is what *Ikigai* is all about – the Japanese concept that means 'a reason for being': creating a life of meaning beyond just work. This woman's job and skill set had been morphing as the world changed, and she had been prepared to disrupt herself by designing financial products instead of dresses, because she really understood who she is.

In another conversation, an investment advisor wrapped up his essence in one sentence: 'I understand human fear and greed, and I can read people; I can apply this understanding in many different ways, and I currently choose to help people with their investments.' Now here is a man who understands what he is inherently good at and is open to the fact that he will be able to apply his passion, knowledge and skill set to other jobs in the future. He does not have a fixed mindset about what his job needs to look like, but realises that he must put his strengths to work.

CREATING A LIFE OF MEANING

There are more people on our planet today wanting to create a life of meaning than ever before, and many search in vain for this meaning their whole lives long. Millennials are typical examples of this, and so are Boomers who are reaching the second half of their lives and searching for meaning beyond work. Semantics are actually very important in this regard. Perhaps we need to use different words to solve the conundrum that vexes so many people.

In the words of scholar, writer and teacher Joseph Campbell: 'People say that what we're seeking is a meaning for life. I don't think that's what we're really seeking. I think that what we're seeking is an experience of being alive, so that our life experiences on the purely physical plane will have resonance within our innermost being and reality, so that we are able to feel the rapture of being alive.'[25]

Campbell asserts that people throughout the ages, no matter their religious or mystical traditions, are not really searching for a way to save the world or for enlightenment. All they want is to really feel alive and connected in a deep way. I call this having a sense of belonging and purpose. Campbell adds that if people stumble across a desire to serve humanity or to find God while really engaging with life, then the journey is likely to bear fruit. However, he warns that loving, leading, working or praying from a dry well may result in serving 'a bitter cup' to those around you and never really living the life you were given. To return to how this connects to my husband's death: once I had found a parking place and a purpose for my pain, I could fill my cup again. Life became much easier, and I had even more to offer my audiences.

You don't have to be at the top of a corporate ladder, be famous or change the world to live a meaningful life. What you do need is to create your very own version of happiness and success wherever you happen to be right now instead of measuring yourself against others. We each have a different timeline and must own our personal experience.

I once learnt a very important lesson from my son's swimming coach when he told the class of nine-year-olds that they each needed to find their own stroke rate and rhythm. He made them really think about how their own height and strength, together with the length of the pool, would determine this, and pointed out that their stroke rate may be slightly different to that of the swimmer next to them – and that this was fine. The lesson was that when you compete against others you often lose your own rhythm and focus because you try to take on that of your competitor, but if you stick to your own rhythm and stroke rate and aim to improve on *your* personal best, your successes will be truly worthy of praise. The advice of running your own race is a good lesson for life.

Can you drill down into who you are and the work that you do (which is an expression of who you are) and uncover your essence? I introduce myself to people in a business setting as a speaker and a writer – that's what I do, it's how I express myself. What gets me up in the morning, though, is:

- creating
- teaching
- pulling concepts apart and putting them back together again in a different way
- taking complex topics and making them accessible
- hearing what is not being expressly said and trouble-shooting that
- asking lots of questions.

In essence, I am an analyser, synthesiser, creator and teacher. I can sense patterns and see connections and solutions that others can't. This is what underpins my brand of speaking and writing. It's what clients pay me for. It's what the world needs. It's what I love to do. It's what I am good at, and it's what I take with me wherever I go, in any personal or professional capacity.

The mantra in the world of work today is that who you are is going to be far more important than what you do or what you sell. This will be true because what you do and what you sell is going to keep changing in response to the megatrends and disruptive forces discussed in Part 1 of this book. We will keep having to adapt and adjust as we go.

I encourage you to dig deeper than your job description at home or at work to get closer to the essence of who you are. This is an X factor that will differentiate you from other people, and companies are on the lookout for difference and diversity today.

Takeaways for winning at work

- Who you are is more important than what you do or what you sell
- Have you taken the time to drill down into the essence of who you are and what makes you tick – or are you far too busy for this? Maybe you need to find yourself a muse – your own blue crane (see page 126)
- Have you worked out what gets you up in the morning – what lights your fire?
- Be curious and do some profiling assessments, but bear in mind that these are not the only way to define yourself; they simply help you connect the dots to start building a picture of the different facets of who you are
- Don't let profiling tools predetermine who you are: people are flexible, teachable beings who are always in the process of evolving, changing and growing
- Can you see how you could apply your essence – your unique skill set or the way you think – to a variety of different jobs or industries beyond the job you currently have?
- If you are leading a team, what insights do you have about your team members beyond their job description?

    - Have you had 'get to know you' conversations with team members about who they are, and not only about what they do at work?
    - Are you listening with all your senses when you are around them to pick up clues about matters that may be beyond words?
- Getting to know your team members better will help you deploy people more appropriately for the task or challenge at hand
- Run your own race: always push up against your personal best, not someone else's!

Takeaways for winning at home and life

- Design your own life
- Determine your values and what is important to you – how you spend your time and money will give you clues about your values, which will help you to create a meaningful life
- Raise your family to celebrate not only what each member is able to do, but also who they are by purchasing or making a family celebration plate
    - The person of honour at the dinner table gets to eat off the plate
    - Use it to celebrate achievements when they happen
    - Also use it to celebrate family members for who they are; for example, if your child has been really kind to the new kid in class, celebrate their kindness; if your child has persevered and raised their marks or got themselves promoted to a higher team, celebrate their determination and perseverance
    - Our handmade plate had these words painted on it: We love you; We acknowledge you; We honour you; We treasure you; You are unique; You are special
- You can often see the essence of your family members shining through in unexpected situations and circumstances, so take note
- A family is a team, so I strongly recommend that you do the StandOut® Strengths Assessment, which I mentioned in Chapter 17.[26] There is nothing like some fresh input to start a conversation and create more reasons to bond. It's also good for both you and your children to see beyond the label of parent, son or daughter

Chapter 19

Becoming a Brand of One

The pandemic aside, remote working is set to change the way people are recruited and employed. Entrepreneurs know they have to evolve, stay relevant and deliver to stay in business. If you are currently employed, I urge you to start thinking of yourself as a free agent, and to keep looking for the next opportunity, either within or outside your current organisation. This is something everyone – regardless of profession or vocation – should be doing. Consciously start managing yourself as a Brand of One – in other words, be your own CEO, marketing manager, HR manager, sales manager and financial director.

When you treat yourself as a business, as Brand Me Inc. (replace 'Me' with your own name) and see yourself through each of those different lenses, you take an objective step away from yourself. We tend to be very good at giving our friends and colleagues advice but not so good at following our own. You might make different, or more strategic, decisions about your future if you see yourself as an employee of your own business. This is an important mental shift to make, as we expect companies to employ fewer people full-time in the future and outsource more work on a project basis.

The gig or on-demand economy is the fastest-growing 'employment sector' in the world. In the US alone, freelancing contributed $1.2 trillion in 2020, comparable to that of a major industry like the information sector. In its seventh annual study, Upwork's *Freelance Forward 2020* surveyed 6 000 US workers over the age of eighteen and found that fifty-nine million Americans had performed freelance work in the previous twelve months, representing 36 per cent of the US workforce – an increase of two million freelancers since 2019.[27]

Many businesses will discover, as I have, that they can employ good people on demand on a project basis instead of employing them full-time. Why wouldn't they if there are many additional benefits. To name a few:

- No UIF payments
- No medical aid
- No pension fund
- No employee assistance programme services to fund
- No retrenchment packages
- Smaller offices with work stations, or no real estate at all
- Lower maintenance and catering costs
- Fewer people employed in core areas such as finance and human resources.

So how do you future-proof yourself for such a world? The answer is that you consciously create yourself as a standout, unique Brand of One. This has nothing to do with being a celebrity. Rather, it is all about understanding who you are and why you do what you do. What is your skill set? Do you deliver on time? Can you be trusted? Is your work of high quality? Are you constantly upgrading your skills and knowledge to be relevant? What problems can you solve for clients (your current employer, or external clients)?

Entrepreneurs have to put a value on their time, otherwise they don't make money. This is a key metric, and one I am helping my eldest son with as he sets himself up in the world of work. He came to me with a proposal for a client without working out the base cost for himself. Now, if you are employed, the company works out its base cost for you before they add profit margin when quoting. You need to start doing the same so that you know your value should you ever want (or need) to pitch for business in your own capacity.

Knowing the value you bring to an organisation or a team – not just the financial value you add, but the gifts you bring to the team – is extremely important, so that you get paid what you deserve and find a job or project that is a good fit. There is nothing worse than feeling you are being underpaid or that your job is a mismatch. If you are in this situation, you need to do some job-crafting to work out how you can turn what you are doing into a meaningful contribution to the Brand of One that you are now consciously creating. The clearer your vision of who you are, what you do, the value you bring and what you want, the more you will start to attract it. If you are not clear about this yourself, the chance of a mismatch is high.

WHY AN ENTREPRENEURIAL MINDSET IS SOUGHT AFTER IN BUSINESS

There is plenty of talk of missing water-cooler conversations and social coffee breaks now that people are working remotely. It is true that many a problem has been solved in the hallways of a company after a meeting while walking back to the office or driving home after a brainstorming session. Great ideas often come to us in unusual places – while we are in the shower, or when we are on holiday, when our minds have time to wander. When I get writer's block, the best thing is to stop and do something completely different, like gardening or having lunch with a friend.

Our brains are smarter than we give them credit for, and they don't necessarily keep office hours. Some characteristics of entrepreneurs and self-employed people that are prized include:

- They don't clock-watch
- They do what it takes to get the job done on time
- They keep coffee breaks and water-cooler conversations to a minimum because there is a job to be done and not a minute to spare, as time is money
- They don't necessarily follow the rules; they sometimes work outside the rules to get things done
- They are prized for their initiative and accountability – they don't wait to be told to get something done.

The message here is not that you have to go and start your own business tomorrow or develop a side hustle, but that you shift your mindset to thinking about yourself differently to start future-proofing yourself. Become an indispensable 'intrapreneur' – an employee with an entrepreneurial mindset – and raise your value within your organisation. Your journey starts with taking a step away from yourself, becoming more objective, and consulting to yourself as if you were a business or a client. It's a neat little trick that has helped many self-employed people and entrepreneurs to keep on top of their game.

Takeaways to help you win at work

- Become a self-directed 'intrapreneur' if you are employed
- Carve out your own path and niche – become known for something within your organisation or in the marketplace
- Become the go-to person for something beyond your job title
- Develop a mobile skill set that you can take wherever you go
- Have a flexible skill set so that you can plug into different parts of the organisation as required
- Invest in yourself, your own learning and your own personal development – and take what you have learnt with you
- Create different income streams to protect you from the tides of change
- To be ready for guaranteed periods of unemployment, make sure you have a side hustle or two to tide you over financially as businesses morph and change
- Be prepared to take sabbaticals – periods of voluntary retirement – to upskill yourself (a thirty-two-year-old colleague of mine took his first planned year off when he turned thirty, and plans to do so every ten years to reinvent himself and stay relevant – knowing that he will work for longer than previous generations did)
- Be savvy about what you are prepared to pay for and what you can do for free to upgrade your skills and knowledge – one qualification will not be sufficient for the longer, multistage lives we are living today (check out what is available for free, from Ivy League universities to platforms such as Coursera and Khan Academy)
- Don't wait for a boss or HR manager to tell you to go and learn something; drive your own learning journey

Takeaways to help you win at home and life

- Live within your means
- Make sure you are saving and investing a portion of your income so that your assets are working for you; you may need them for various reasons:

  - To tide you over when you are upgrading your skill set and qualifications
  - To cover you if you should become unemployed or while doing freelance work between jobs
  - To augment your salary if job sharing becomes a reality for you
- If you are a stay-at-home parent:
  - Develop interests or skills that could generate an income at some stage
  - Research and keep up with market trends in your area of speciality, even if you are not working
  - Make sure you don't fall behind in a fast-changing world
  - Develop the courage to apply skills from one area of your life to another
  - Don't wait to put yourself into the job market before you think you have the perfect skills or know enough: start somewhere, as you might find that it's the stepping stone to the next job!
  - Know that it is easier than ever to get into the gig economy, as you can pitch your skills on platforms such as www.upwork.com (there are many others) to find your feet and do what works for you before taking on a full-time job, becoming a freelancer or building a business from scratch
  - Encourage your teens or young adults to develop a track record of work experience and side hustles, even if that means selling their skills online if they can't find part-time or full-time employment in the real world – it all counts and shows how proactive they are
- Whether you are employed or self-employed, aim to become a standout Brand of One. Then, even if you end up creating a number of different careers – I've had three – you can take your skills, knowledge, your following and your client loyalty wherever you go

Chapter 20

Develop your X factors for success

Regardless of whether you are a business owner or not, you are your own most valuable asset. Keep investing in yourself and your own development. You are way bigger than your qualifications. You are the sum total of all your experiences, your networks, how you think and how you operate in the world. Whatever you are doing, make sure you are developing and recording your X factors for success that go beyond what is captured in a traditional curriculum vitae (CV). They will make for much more interesting reading or discussion in an interview with a future employer, client or potential investor.

X factors add richness, depth and colour. They showcase what can't be quantified or measured. They tell your story, the narrative of your life so far. Don't underestimate the importance of this, as more companies hire for attitude and train for skills. Businesses who have led the charge include the likes of Ernst & Young, Facebook, LinkedIn, Google and Amazon. Leadership expert, author and TED speaker Simon Sinek says he loves to hire great people and then put them in positions they are not qualified for. By throwing them into the unexpected, by disrupting them, both he and they get to see their real depth of talent and resourcefulness.

Here are some of the key X factors you should be capturing from your personal and professional experiences that will make you stand out from others:

- Creativity
  - How do you think outside the box?
  - What innovative solutions have you created?
  - Can you showcase examples of your critical-thinking and problem-
  - solving skills?
- Resilience and resourcefulness
  - How do you bounce back from adversity?

- How do you cope with change?
- Can you make a plan when facing a challenge?
- How flexible are you?
- Do you display grit, perseverance and persistence?

- Being a committed learner
  - Are you able and willing to learn, unlearn and relearn?
  - Do you take charge of your own learning journey?
  - Do you put yourself through courses voluntarily?
  - Are you constantly upskilling to remain relevant and employable?
  - Do you have good general knowledge?
  - Do you keep up to date on trends that affect your industry?
  - What are you reading?
- Communication
  - Can you communicate your ideas and thoughts clearly?
  - Can you sell your ideas?
  - What value do you bring to a team?
  - How good are your online and offline communication skills?
  - What are your writing skills like?
  - How good are you at negotiation?
- Self-knowledge
  - How well do you know yourself?
  - What profiling tools have you used?
  - Under what conditions do you get your best work done?
  - What are your strengths?
  - What are your weaknesses?
  - How do you behave under stress and pressure?

I encourage you to record your X factors, stories, experiences and continuing development over time in a talent profile – a multimedia report card of life that goes beyond the biographical, demographic, academic and employment information contained in a traditional CV (which is now a rather outdated concept). The talent-profile concept was introduced in one of my earlier books, *Future-proof Your Child*, and applies just as much to experienced adults today as it does to young professionals and teens. In short, a talent profile should include:

- Biographical information
- Your academic record
- Work experience with contact details for references
- Talents (strengths)
- Interests
- Skills (what you can actually do)
- Character attributes (for example, a high need to care)
- Personal examples of the five X factors for success detailed above
- Multimedia items such as videos, podcasts or photographs, or links to these
- Links to personal websites or blogs (blogs are a good way to showcase your interests, depth of knowledge and opinions)
- Links to social media profiles
- Links to any information on projects or endeavours that are available online
- Multimedia referrals and recommendations from people (teachers, lecturers, clients, employers, friends, family, LinkedIn contacts, and so on).

A talent profile differs from a CV because it showcases the essence of who you are, your uniqueness, and points of difference from others with similar qualifications or experience. It shows self-knowledge and self-awareness which, in turn, shows emotional intelligence. You want to get your personality and character across. You need to learn how to brand, package and market yourself as a valuable asset – as a distinctive Brand of One that becomes more interesting every day.

Really start to examine what you do and the value you bring to your organisation, and do so on a regular basis. You may not think so now, but I promise you that at some time in the future it will come in handy. A teacher walked up to me at a conference recently and thanked me for inspiring her four years earlier to capture her X factors and her talent profile. She decided she wanted to switch lanes and become an IT teacher, but had no experience or specific qualification for this position whatsoever, so she specifically used technology to present herself in the job application and interview, while all the other applicants simply submitted a written CV. Guess who got the job?

JOB INTERVIEW QUESTIONS

Many candidates who make it to a face-to-face job interview after going through the initial online application and elimination rounds might have the same qualifications. Interviewers are therefore looking for differentiators, and you may well be asked to:

- Showcase an innovative solution
- Demonstrate your commitment to your own learning journey
- Give examples of your ability to be resilient in tough times
- Show how resourceful you are
- Indicate how well you know yourself; for example, what unique skills you would bring to a team, or what your best work environment is, and what profiling you have done to get to know yourself better
- Showcase examples of how you have worked in teams in the real and virtual worlds.

The aim of a talent profile isn't simply to get you a job or a position; it ensures that the job on offer is a good fit for you *and* for the company doing the recruiting. After all, companies need to create teams that work, and individuals want to create a life of meaning beyond a job for money. This means expressing yourself through work that is meaningful to you, and hence it needs to be a good fit. The Japanese concept of *Ikigai* I referred to in Chapter 18 (see page 140) encompasses the idea that to live a fulfilled life you should not only be doing what you are good at or what someone will pay you to do, but also do what you love and what will make a difference in the world.

There is a heap of good talent out there, so be sure to convey what makes you special or distinct.

IS YOUR CURRENT JOB HELPING YOU TO DEVELOP YOUR X FACTORS?

Do you ever ask yourself whether the job you are doing right now is bolstering your talent profile to make you more employable or valuable? When you are finished where you are, what must you be able to add to your talent profile? Do you have a realistic and clear idea of what your takeaway from your current job experience needs to be when you leave? Are you working towards that? Does your boss know what a meaningful experience for you needs to look like?

I am not suggesting you demand anything, but I am encouraging you to create a win–win scenario. What does your boss need you to do to help them deliver on their key performance indicators, and what can they help you to achieve in terms of enriching your experience or developing your X factors for success while you are with them? You will rarely land up in a perfect job. What is important is that each job or project you work on provides you with an opportunity to add something worthwhile to your talent profile. This outcome should create a sense of satisfaction all on its own and help you see your job differently – not as work you do simply for money, but as a vehicle for personal development and self-expression too.

A talent profile is useful, no matter whether you are in the early, middle or late stages of your working life. Even people who are nearing retirement will need a talent profile as they refire for the next stage of life – which is unlikely to be retirement as we know it. Your profile might make for good reading by your children and grandchildren one day too! It tells your story, tracks your journey and showcases your evolution.

Beyond a report card and certifications, what sets one person apart from another? This really boils down to who you are, why you do the things you do and how you operate in the world. Don't miss an opportunity to capture your X factors before you forget where you've been and what you've done. It's an opportunity for self-reflection – something that all successful people take the time to do. The X factor really is YOU!

Takeaways for winning at work

- When last did you update your CV?
- If you are still relying on a conventional CV, it's time to create your talent profile so that you are mission-ready should the need arise for something more substantial than a CV
- Capture the development of your X factors over time
- Keep adding to the record so that there is always something current while you are amassing experience
- Your X factors make you stand out and differentiate you from another candidate with the same qualifications
- Become aware of the need to develop your awareness of your X factors and start to consciously fill in any gaps – find ways to create

them in your current job or position to make you more valuable when applying for a new job or promotion
- Ask your boss or colleague for their input; you may have blind spots about yourself and not see the value you are already bringing
- A talent profile is a sales and marketing tool, and you are the product – Brand Me Inc.
- Don't lose any opportunity to get testimonials or referrals from people you have worked with – if you leave it too long, you will forget or lose contact with that person; this includes getting referrals on LinkedIn

Takeaways for winning at home and life

- Never underestimate the value of how you lead and manage your home team
- Stay-at-home parents should not discount the X factors they are developing that will be valuable in a job
- Help every family member from the age of eight upwards to develop and record their X factors
    - You never know when they might come in handy – whether for a spot on a team, a leadership position or even some seed funding
    - Play 'Spot the X factor' once a week as a family with children and young adults
    - Help each other to spot X factors worth recording
- What you think isn't an X factor might be really important – sometimes we are just a bit too close to ourselves to see it
- Incorporate your X factors into a talent profile
- Think of a talent profile as a multimedia scrapbook of your life – far more than a CV, it's a celebration of who you are, where you have been and all the experience you bring to the table
- It's proof of your journey in both work and life and the value you add in all your different roles
- Use it to affirm yourself and feel proud of who you are

Chapter 21

Shift your perspective on purpose

When last did you do something counter-intuitive or disruptive to shift your perspective on purpose? In an era of deep change, we must find ways to help our brains to learn, unlearn and relearn to stay flexible and open to doing things differently. Remember that your brain is a muscle that can be trained. It's neuroplastic, so it's always able to learn. Human beings are complex, adaptive systems. This means we are constantly adapting to our environment, shifting and changing, and able to meet the needs of the environment, as long as we remain flexible and don't get stuck. Actually, getting stuck is not the problem; staying stuck is.

You must challenge long-held assumptions and practise shifting perspective to train your brain. You can do this in some very simple ways. Some of my recent shifts in perspective or my view of the world have come from:

- Sleeping on the other side of the bed to the side I am used to
    - This is a small thing to do, but it does prove a point: you see things in the room differently, you might feel a little different too, and the experience unleashed some ideas for this book
- Moving to a new suburb
    - You get used to one place (ask me: I lived in the same house for twenty-three years)
    - Everything is comfortable and familiar
    - You don't have to think about the routes you drive; you do so automatically
    - When you move, you have to rewire your brain and learn new routes because nothing is familiar
    - You have to stretch yourself
    - It is uncomfortable for a while (especially when your new pharmacist

doesn't know who you are or what your address is when you are used to them knowing the particulars of your life)

- Shopping in different shops
    - When I travel I love visiting shops that are different to those I know
    - Choosing a new shopping centre in a different suburb achieves the same goal (although local chain stores do provide an element of continuity)
    - Novelty and newness has its place in disrupting our automatic processes and preferences
    - If you want to save money, however, it is best to always go to the same supermarket, because any change in layout will make you look at and consider buying stuff you don't need
- Walking my normal route in reverse
    - If you are a runner or walker, try doing your route the other way round
    - You will see everything differently
    - You will spot things you don't usually see (in fact, you might think you are on a different route entirely!)
    - The change will give your brain and sensory system a good wake-up
- Using the non-dominant hand
    - This is something you wouldn't necessarily choose to do if you didn't have to
    - My son's friend, who had cancer, lost his dominant hand when his arm had to be amputated just above the elbow. This determined young sportsman's life was changed forever, but within six weeks of the operation he had taught himself how to write and colour in with his left hand; he has since become a single-handed golfer and simply gets on with his life, rarely asking for help. He is an amazing testament to the ability of the brain to rewire itself in response to change.
- Taking my business 100 per cent online
    - To begin with, this was as foreign to me as it might be to you, but now it's become almost normal for me
- Four weeks of initial disruption involved
    - Losing all my real-world speaking bookings for 2020

  - Learning how to use new equipment and unearthing audiovisual equipment I owned but had never used
  - Learning how to use a virtual platform I had invested in for years but had never activated; this enabled me to host an unlimited number of delegates for webinar presentations
  - Learning how to use different virtual conferencing platforms (VCs) – at last count I'd used eighteen different VCs in the first eight months of the pandemic
  - Late nights speaking to other professionals in my field to troubleshoot issues I was grappling with
  - Drawing up new client agreements for the virtual space
  - Creating new content for a new time: presentations, white papers, blogs, social media posts, marketing material, launching a podcast
- Now, virtual is normal. As with anything, we have to keep asking ourselves how we are going to up our game, create more value and continue to build our Brand of One.

WHY YOU FEEL INCOMPETENT AND UNCONFIDENT

When you start out doing anything differently or something new, you are likely to feel incompetent and unconfident. Didn't you feel at sea for quite a long time when you were sent home to work? Maybe you still feel that way. This happens quite literally because the neurological pathway in your brain for that thought or action doesn't exist yet or hasn't been well established. Think about walking up a hill in thick long grass where no one has been before. It's tough; there is resistance; there is no pathway. You wade through and stumble on the uneven ground. But once the hundredth or thousandth person walks the same way, a well-worn path begins to emerge and access to the hill becomes easier and easier.

The brain reacts to new experiences in the same way. The more you entertain the same thought or repeat the same action, the more a fatty substance called myelin is laid down on the neurological pathway, making the electrical impulses that move through the pathway fire faster and more efficiently. That's why repetition is such an important component in learning anything new. Without repetition, we forget. Repetition makes things become automatic, and we no longer default to our old 'settings' and ways of being and doing things.

Disruption calls us to change, to do and think differently, regardless of whether we are experiencing a disrupted relationship, a business that needs to pivot due to new technology or shifting markets, or adapting to working from home because of lockdown restrictions. It requires rewiring our brains and taking on the challenge of learning, unlearning and relearning, or risk landing up being the illiterates of the twenty-first century – as Alvin Toffler, author of *Future Shock*, aptly put it. To remain relevant, we must keep up and dance with disruptive forces in our lives.

Takeaways for winning at work

- Push your team to do What If™ scenario planning to prepare team members for new ways of thinking and doing in your industry or your division
  - Considering possibilities opens up the mind to new ways of doing things and will prepare you for the future
- Once a quarter, let your team members choose a book for a teammate to read that they are least likely to choose for themselves
  - This allows you to reset your default thinking patterns
  - We are such creatures of habit that we love to go down the same tunnel over and over again. While this is comfortable, it also reinforces the same thinking patterns and does not help us expand our world view
- Use team building, team bonding and team development sessions as opportunities create new experiences and perspectives

Takeaways for winning at home and life

- Children can have wacky ideas, and they challenge how we do things and think about them
  - If your child wants to put tomato sauce on their cornflakes instead of milk, what's the harm in trying?
  - My nephew went through a phase of wearing outrageous patterned socks with shorts. I can see my mom (his gran) screwing up her face in disapproval. I, by contrast, am quite

comfortable that he is going through a phase of making a statement that he is his own person. It is a stage that'll pass

- Puzzle-building shows us how we all think differently
    - Some people build with a system by finding corners and building the outside frame first, while others find a picture within the puzzle and start there
    - Learn to appreciate diversity in thinking and approaches, starting in your own home
- Teach children that there are certain rules that need to be kept and obeyed for our safety and to benefit society, but there are times when challenging or breaking the rules is okay
- Shifting your perspective on purpose is a great way to dance with disruption. Try it!

PART 5

LEADING YOUR TEAM AT WORK AND HOME

Everyone has different reference points for leading their work team and their home team. Whether you are leading a team at work, leading your family at home or leading yourself, it's all leadership and it's all parenting. The way we lead both teams, however, should be consistent. How you do anything should be how you do everything. When I work with organisations, I always use my parenting analogy: Whoever we are and wherever we are, we are all contributing to raising talent and human potential, helping those around us to future-proof themselves. In the process, as we journey together, we are helping ourselves too.

I am well aware that many people are battling with work–life balance (pre-pandemic and now) precisely because they see themselves as separate people at home and at work that are disconnected from each other. I strongly believe that home and work merely provide different avenues for self-expression. One of the core pillars of my work is to help individuals to see themselves as one integrated person who is able to bring their whole self to the table at home and at work, *and* who is consistent in both teams.

In 2013 I shared a speaking platform with cricketing legend Gary Kirsten, who discussed the parallels between leading, parenting and coaching a cricket team. He explained that these parallels helped him be consistent in his career and on the home front with his three children. He listed these characteristics:

- be credible
- be trustworthy
- be compassionate
- be consistent
- be an inspiration
- be a good listener
- be a good example.

Isn't it interesting that Gary's list is about being and not doing? He believes that who you are has a huge bearing on how you lead, parent and coach other people in your sphere of influence. He recounted how, when he started coaching the Indian cricket team, he had zero hours of coaching experience: 'I remember asking myself, "What do I have to offer?" Especially when Sachin Tendulkar is going to ask me about his batting, and I think he knows everything he needs to know about his batting! Then I thought to myself: What I can offer is all of myself, as a human being. Then the big question was: "Will that be enough?" It's the same when it comes to parenting, and so it really boils down to how I live out the concepts on this list, every day, in front of my children and the people I lead.'

Gary tells of a parenting wake-up call he had when bowling to his son James, who was four years old at the time – while Gary was spending hundreds of days away from his family each year as the Proteas cricket coach. 'James was batting quite nicely, although I noticed that he was holding his cricket bat like golfing Masters winner Adam Scott! I suggested that perhaps he should change the position of his left hand if he wanted to carry on a career in cricket, to which he said, "No, Dad, you don't know what you are talking about!"' This was a clear indicator to Gary that he needed to spend more time at home to re-establish his credibility!

Gary's story is a reminder that none of us are perfect parents or leaders, but we can all work on ourselves and be the best we can in ways that count – each and every day – even when we are not with our children or our teams. Keep this thought in mind, both as a parent and a leader at work: success means writing yourself out of your job because those you lead become so competent that they can work independently of you and succeed without you. Aiming for redundancy seems counter-intuitive, but it is where you need to head to future-proof those around you. Lead them to competence, confidence and independence.

EXERCISE: YOUR LEADERSHIP TRAITS

Can you think of situations and examples from the past week or two in which you demonstrated any of these leadership traits to your children and your colleagues at work?

LEADERSHIP TRAIT	FAMILY	WORK
Trustworthiness		
Compassion		
Consistency/fairness		
Good listening skills		
Being a positive role model		

As a leader, you are there to serve your team. This means you need to bring your whole self to the table – head and heart. Help your team members carry out their roles to the best of their ability. Serve them, and they will serve you. Here's how you can serve your team:

- Be the leader they need to see in the world
- Teams with good leaders produce sustainable results
- Remember that as much as you are a leader, you are also a team member
- Everyone is looking for a sense of belonging and togetherness
- Satisfaction comes not just from meeting goals and key performance indicators but from seeing your team thriving at work and at home
- Give your team reasons to have confidence in you
- Trust is built consistently over time and through repetitive actions
- Listen to your team – *really* listen.

As a parent you are there to serve your family. This means bringing the leadership traits you apply at work into the family environment. Inspire your family to become successful team members who do what they can to contribute to the family team.

- The art of effective parenting is learning how to be fully emotionally present when you are with your children
- Remember that children learn from what they see, so lead by example
- Listen to them – to the words they speak, to the meaning behind the words and to what is not being said
- Really *see* the members of your family – not only their physical bodies, but everything they are and all of their potential
- Your job is to raise them up and then set them free.

We do not travel this life alone. Human beings are social creatures who need to connect with one another, feel part of a community, be supported and support others. We are members of a team at home, we have friends in life, and we have our work team too. Within the 'we' of a team we discover the 'me' when others act as mirrors for us.

Belonging and togetherness is a fundamental human need. We want to share our experiences with others and be part of something bigger than ourselves – a team, a cause, a story. Human beings are essentially social creatures, and we do better when we find our tribe. The tribe can be the family, a group of friends, an interest group, or colleagues and teams at work.

Collaborating with others and working as a team can bring a sense of enormous satisfaction. 'Together we can do more' is about creating a healthy symbiosis (not a dependency) that allows us to help each other succeed and grow. In the process, the whole team wins. We need to support each other through good times and bad, while always encouraging each other to grow and improve, to become more than we were yesterday. In times of crisis, we walk a fine line between rescuing and empowering each other while co-creating the future.

Chapter 22

Don't rescue others – empower them

Too often, we rush in to save someone who is going through a tough time. We want to take the pain or stress away. We are wired to help others when things go wrong, and to commiserate. It's called empathy, and the world needs lots of it. But be careful, because you may unwittingly, despite your good intentions, trap them in a victim space.

Being supportive is one thing; playing the saviour or rescuer too often can rob the other person – adult or child – of the opportunity to develop their problem-solving muscle to empower them to handle life and stressful situations. In essence, they have to develop the belief that they can do this for themselves – an essential part of acquiring grit, resilience and hope.

Aim to help others to develop their problem-solving muscle instead of rescuing them. Support them in developing emotional resilience and stress-management skills for themselves. Lead your family and your team to empowerment, not dependency.

Have you ever considered how rescuing others can actually minimise them and make them feel smaller and less competent? I have experienced this feeling. Have you? We can help and empower others more by acknowledging the challenge and responding with something like this: 'It may not be something you want (or want to go through), but I think it's something you can handle.' This helps them build their problem-solving muscle, whether we are talking about your colleagues, life partner, a friend or your kids.

While this is a statement, it is far more than that. It's passing on your belief in that person's ability to rise above the immediate challenge to learn and grow from it, instead of you micromanaging them and wrapping them in cotton wool.

Life happens, and not everything is in our control. Some things happen that we like, or that we want for ourselves. Sometimes we create these things, or we create perfect conditions in which we are able to flourish. Other things happen that we wouldn't necessarily choose, but which we can handle. Sometimes life hits us with a crisis, such as Covid-19. Such situations require us to tap into both internal and external resources to cope with sideswipes we weren't expecting. But these situations have the potential to change us and allow us to grow. However, growth requires:

- courage
- emotional resilience
- problem-solving and solution-finding abilities
- the ability to reframe our thinking
- choosing to re-author the script of our lives.

Nothing on this list is easy, but everything is doable if we choose to go that route. Without a doubt, someone who sees the glass as half full is more inclined to see the positive opportunities in a negative situation. They consciously ask themselves these questions and this energises their will to move forward:

- How can I use this challenge to become more resilient?
- What skill or lesson can I learn from this challenge that will help me in future?
- How is this situation helping me to see myself differently, or shift my perspective about myself?
- How is this challenge helping me to develop my X factors for success to enrich my talent profile?

If you are managing a family or a team in your business, it is your responsibility as a leader and entrepreneur to encourage and empower them to learn how to solve problems for themselves. This enables them to develop their personal leadership skills, their resilience and their problem-solving muscle.

In fact, as I wrote in the introduction, one of the keys to effective leadership is to work yourself out of a job. If you do your job well, and raise those beneath you up, you should be able to move on, and the business or the department should be able to operate without you. The same goes for your children: the ultimate goal of parenting is to let your children go so that they can create their own version of happiness and success independently, without you.

When dealing with family stress at home or a team member's stress at work, always remember that your goal should be to empower instead of rescuing someone – to shape solution seekers, not problem finders. In the long run, this approach will be in your team members' own best interests, as well as yours!

If you keep rescuing your friends, your children, your partner or your team members, they develop a state that is known as learned helplessness. Empower them instead by helping them to develop their own problem-solving muscle. Life is a series of problems to be solved – a continuous series of Mystery Box Challenges (see Chapter 16). Help them spot and solve these challenges. They will be so grateful in the long run, and it will save you time and energy.

Takeaways for winning at work

- Be a good coach: don't rescue your team members but empower them instead
- You are only the guide – and guiding is the trademark of an effective manager and leader
- Listen to others! You are not the only one with solutions or ideas that can transform your business in this disruptive time
- Help your team members to become solution seekers rather than problem finders

Takeaways for winning at home and life

- In essence, parents need to be coaches too
- Stay calm and offer a measured response (remember to manage your own stress and you will help others learn how to manage theirs too)
- Listen, don't lecture
- Children need more conversations that matter and fewer speeches that don't
- Don't always rescue your children when they face obstacles or deal with difficult relationships, as these provide real opportunities for meaningful learning
    - When they ask what they should do, first reflect the question back at them: 'What do you think you should do?'

- Keep asking questions in response to their questions instead of giving answers (this is known as the Socratic method)
- Help them drill down into how they think they could handle the situation or solve the problem: 'I like the way you are thinking. But have you thought about this?/Perhaps that could work.' The aim is to keep the conversation going
- Guide them to find their own solutions, which they will be able to implement and then own. This will go a long way towards helping them develop an 'I can' philosophy, which will stand them in good stead as they successfully move towards independence as they grow up

Chapter 23

Are you really listening?

'The fundamental cause of nearly all communication problems is that people don't listen to understand; they listen to reply.' This insight from leadership experts John Maxwell and Les Parrott hit me right between the eyes.[28] It refers to a classic trap we all fall into regularly, especially when we are stressed or under time pressure.

My husband used to tell me I was particularly guilty of this, often completing his sentences before he even finished what he had to say. He was right. How often do we jump to conclusions before our children complete their often slow and meandering explanation of what happened to them on the playground, how they fell short in a test, or when they are spilling the beans about a friendship break-up? How many of us are really listening to our colleagues during meetings as we fight for airtime to be seen and recognised, and to stand out ourselves?

Conversation is actually a really poor form of communication precisely because we are listening with the intention to reply to the other person rather than really dropping fully into the present and hearing them. We are always in the process of moving beyond this conversation to a solution, sometimes missing the point, making the person who is speaking feel sidelined.

We mistakenly prioritise expressing our own ideas and feelings instead of giving people what they want in a communication transaction – to be heard, respected and understood. This is a skill we all need to learn, but it is particularly important if you are leading a team in business or raising a family.

This means listening not only to what is being said, but to what is 'between the lines'. It means tuning in and listening with your heart, not only your ears. Maxwell calls this 'listening aggressively'.[29] I call it 'listening with intention', to hear not only the words, but to what is *not* being said. It requires you to be fully present, in the moment, whether you are communicating with your child, your partner, a friend or a colleague at work. Strategies for listening intentionally with both your ears and your heart are:

- Disconnect from technological distractions
- Be open and not defensive
- Be curious: you don't have all the answers, and you may be surprised
- Don't jump to conclusions
- Try to understand where the other person is coming from.

According to Caspar Craven, author of *Be More Human*, 'There is little that is more powerful (and rare) in this world than for someone else to give you their undivided attention and for you to feel seen, listened to, understood and heard. The acid test is to demonstrate that understanding by acting on it. It can start with the simple idea of just saying back to someone what you've heard them say. That is rare in itself. Trust builds when you actually act upon what you've heard, doing something deliberate and specific that shows that you really understand what is important to them. By showing that you really care.'[30]

There is great truth in the old adage that people don't care how much you know until they know how much you care. If you really care and you want to make your child, spouse, partner, colleague, team member or boss feel respected and validated, then unclog your ears and open your heart. Listen with your whole being. That's real listening!

It takes some practise to listen with intention, but it's well worth it for the connectedness, engagement and idea generation that result. Learning how to listen well in teams is Communication 101 – an essential part of training. Bear in mind that you have two ears and one mouth, so you should listen twice as much as you speak.

Takeaways for winning at work

- Manage your use of devices when you are with colleagues; nothing breaks a moment of presence like the interruption of a beeping cellphone
- Take a step back: stop trying to compete in a conversation and just

listen with your whole self – and feel the difference

- When you have some time, try a different type of communication: allow each party an agreed-upon uninterrupted time of, for example, ten minutes, during which they hold the floor without any interruptions or responses. Then you get to do the same, not to reply to them, but to put your thoughts, feelings and ideas on the table. Only after that do you go into conversation. This way, no one is competing for airtime and there is more clarity to thoughts and ideas, as nothing interrupts the constructive thinking phase
- When people understand the process and that they are guaranteed a turn, they relax because they are not preoccupied by waiting and trying to spot a gap for inserting themselves. They know they will have their opportunity to get a say
- Create a positive and supportive thinking environment to get the best out of your team by:
    - Paying attention
    - Listening with clear respect and without interruption
    - Giving team members equal opportunity to think and speak; this provides freedom from internal urgency driven by the thought 'will I get a turn to speak?'
- It is not IQ, education, experience or power that enables people to think clearly and creatively, it is the way they are treated by those they are with when they are thinking that is most important – it's about creating an environment that is conducive to creativity
- We make time to think, brainstorm and communicate, but we need to change the way we treat each other while we do these things to get the best results – it shows that we value people and their ideas, and that our way is not the only way
- If you pay attention when you listen instead of listening to respond, you catalyse your thinking
- Practise reflective listening to ensure you understood what was said – 'What I heard you say was … Is that correct?' There is so much room in communication for misinterpretation because we are all subjective listeners coming from our own point of view, with our

own filters and perspective of the world. Instead, check with the person that you understood what they said. A great resource is communication and relationship expert Leah Sefor's book *That's Not What I Meant!* for a crash course in good communication

Takeaways for winning at home and life

- Our kids are full of thoughts, feelings, great ideas and their own experiences of the world
- The more receptive you are, the more they will share
- The more they share, the more they trust you
- The more they trust you, the deeper and stronger your relationship will be
- The stronger your relationship, the more likely they will be to turn to you in times of uncertainty or crisis – you want to be their first port of call, no matter what
- You want them to continue to share their amazing ideas with you, so engage with them instead of shooting them down
- You need to be the empathic listener who reflects their feelings and their situation back at them and empowers them to find their own solution most of the time
- The best way to persuade your children is to listen to them – they will respect you and your opinions far more than if you lecture them without listening
- Don't fall into the trap of wanting to rescue them all the time; this will create dependence and hinder independence
- Manage your devices when you communicate with family members. You seldom have much face-to-face time, so avoid taking calls, especially when something important is happening. Your family needs to feel that they are at the top of your priority list

Chapter 24

Get that Happy Juice flowing

Whether they are employed or self-employed, more people on the planet are in search of meaning than ever before. Something that millennials have brought into sharp focus is that there must be more to life than just work. I am grateful to them for this. We need to find meaning in the life we create for ourselves, which consists of both life at the office and life outside the office. For too long we have compartmentalised our lives and lived as if we were two different people. I have long promoted the notion that we are not – that work and home are merely different avenues of self-expression.

The shift to work from home is providing many people with an opportunity, for the first time, to see the possibility of a more integrated life over which they actually have more control. While working from home is the current reality, it will become working from anywhere when restrictions ease, and we will see rigid adherence to the nine-to-five workday and the five-day work week fall away too.

Companies will pay for someone with skills, expertise and the right attitude to get the job done on time and to the required standard. It will be none of their business what you do with the rest of your time. You will not be answerable for that any more. If you do the job well, what you do with the rest of your time is up to you – whether you play with your kids, go for a run, take a nap, work for another client or create a side hustle. So there will be an incentive to be efficient and to manage time effectively. Hence employees will display higher levels of engagement and productivity as the workplace becomes more output- than input-driven.

But what is Happy Juice? In any endeavour there are a few things that need to be present for us to feel that the reward justifies every bit of effort we put in. After all, we are trading our energy, time, skills and knowledge for a return.

Happy Juice is a simple concept shared with me by Mark Hosking, head of Emerging Technologies in the CEMEA region at international open-source giant Red Hat. He is also the brain behind the Success Cube™ licensed concept I work with when coaching individuals and teams.

Happy Juice comprises reward, satisfaction, value and progression (RSVP). As an individual you can measure your level of Happy Juice in your current job. If you are a manager or team leader, look at each team member through this lens and you will get an answer straight away about their level of Happy Juice:

- Reward
  - Am I being paid decent money for what I do?
- Satisfaction
  - Do I get a feeling of satisfaction from the job I am doing? We often yearn for success without feeling satisfaction along the way, which is an empty way to live.
- Value
  - Am I valued by others/the business?
  - Am I validated and affirmed?
  - Do I value myself?
- Progression
  - Am I growing and learning?
  - Am I improving?
  - Am I becoming more employable?
  - Am I becoming more valuable?

When Happy Juice is flowing, people feel empowered, and their levels of engagement and productivity are high. Until Covid-19 came along, we were seeing desperately low levels of employee engagement and productivity internationally. According to Gallup's *State of the Workplace* report, that figure stands at a low 15 per cent. With the majority of the workforce around the world either viewing their workplace negatively or doing only the bare minimum to make it through the day, with little to no emotional attachment (meaning), no wonder human resources departments were losing sleep.[31]

Bestselling business author Daniel Pink has this to say in his book *Drive: The Surprising Truth About What Motivates Us*:

> Unfortunately, despite sweet-smelling words like "empowerment" that waft through corporate corridors, the modern workplace's most notable feature may be its lack of engagement and its disregard for mastery … The cost of all this disengagement in the US amounts to about US$ 300 billion a year in lost productivity – a sum larger than the GDP of Portugal, Singapore and Israel. [32]

Somehow, our complex management and leadership systems have a fundamental fault. Basic human connection and motivation are lacking. But let's get back to Mark Hosking, who started his career as a teacher, then went into sales, and now builds highly agile teams around the world who launch emerging technologies and systems into business. I really support and enjoy his simple approach, combined with his depth of knowledge about people and what makes them tick. The RSVP formula is a barometer of the emotional temperature of an employee. The word *emotion* in this description should not be ignored: we are, after all, emotional beings at heart, and that is what makes us different to machines. When it comes to future-proofing ourselves, our emotions are one of our biggest strengths and one of our greatest weaknesses, depending on how they are managed.

During the pandemic there has been an interesting rise in employee engagement and productivity, since many people have shifted to working from home. I think it is worth looking at what might be behind it. Dipstick polling research I conducted during my virtual presentations with organisations I worked with in the past year showed a rise to 70–80 per cent employee engagement versus previous figures of around 10–15 per cent. From my perspective, there seem to be four main drivers at play here.

DRIVER #1: FEAR

Fear is an unbelievably powerful motivator. In the case of Covid-19, there is the threat of companies not surviving, of having to downsize and possibly outsource staff instead of employing a large complement of full-time workers. The result has been:

- People putting in extra hours to adjust to working online
- Employees needing to prove that they are necessary to the company in case the firm is thinking of retrenching

- Staff needing to prove their value now that no one can see them – they don't like to feel invisible
- Some people are finally doing the job they were being paid to do, but with more appreciation and commitment, as they actually have a job in times of high unemployment.

While people are no longer spending hours commuting to work, they have replaced that time – and more – with time in front of their computers. Work–life balance now means something completely different in an environment that has no physical demarcation, as work and life now take place in the same space. However, fear is not a sustainable motivator, as it leads to fatigue and burnout.

DRIVER #2: FEELING OUT OF CONTROL

The pandemic brought with it the removal of choice or autonomy because of the many restrictions that were imposed on going to the office, school or shops; which parts of the economy would open up and when; travel; how late you could be out; whether you could buy alcohol or cigarettes; wearing of masks; socialising, and much more. These restrictions have made people feel out of control. One of the first things we do when we feel this way is to try to regain control. Often we then default to over-control. We grip the steering wheel until our knuckles turn white! The results of this have been:

- overwork
- loss of work–life balance
- increased stress levels
- increased levels of depression
- immobilisation – being frozen in fear and unable to take action or work effectively
- raised levels of adrenalin and cortisol.

DRIVER #3: THE NEED FOR ATTENTION

Human beings want to be noticed. When you physically go into the office, you receive acknowledgement that you exist. When people do not have to physically show up, many begin to feel invisible or insignificant. Human beings do strange things to attract attention, even using negative attention-seeking behaviours, which include:

- overwork
- illness
- confrontational behaviour
- withdrawal
- playing the victim
- bullying tactics
- blaming and shaming others
- moodiness.

Do any of the above ring true for you or anyone you work with?

DRIVER #4: THE NEED FOR MASTERY

The shift to working from home was a first for many organisations and individuals who had never done so before. It has provided a logistical nightmare for many businesses. First of all, for the first time, many had to ensure that their employees have the necessary hardware and connectivity to work from home, and deal with challenges around cybersecurity and the use of virtual platforms for information sharing. However, it has put us all on a learning journey which, while challenging, has actually led to growth in many quarters. We didn't realise how adaptable and teachable we were until we had to make this happen – literally overnight.

As an individual concerned with your own future, ask yourself: Am I growing in mastery? Am I becoming more employable? To answer these two questions, start with these points:

- Exploration
    - Is what I am doing leading to personal growth?
    - Am I learning new skills and acquiring new knowledge?
- Mastery
    - We want to know we are making progress, and that we are getting better at something
    - What does excellence look like in what I am doing, and am I getting closer to excellence?

    - A sense of excellence fuels a sense of personal satisfaction for the effort expended and encourages us to do more
- Individual meaning
    - Is what I am doing meaningful to me?
    - Am I getting customised training and motivation?
    - How does what I do in my role contribute to the vision for the organisation?
- Motivation
    - Does what I am doing motivate me?
    - Am I being seen or noticed in my organisation?
    - What do I need to do to be noticed?
    - Am I being affirmed and validated by others in what I do?
- Personal ambition
    - Is what I am doing taking me closer to my perceived purpose or personal ambition?
    - Is the company or are the people I am working with supporting, guiding and leading me closer to my ambition?

Fear is not a sustainable driver of engagement and productivity in the long term. We need a different source of fuel. Our strength will be based on our curiosity about what could be. Both employers and employees need to go back to basics and become more aware of the ingredients for Happy Juice. Then they need to strategise how to ensure that these conditions come into existence in the workplace. That is the job of a leader.

Takeaways for winning at work

- Always remember to put the human in the middle – human beings come before process and profit
- Ask questions, even if you might not want to know the answers
- Listen – really listen – to what people say and how they say it
- You need to dig below the surface to find out what your team members really need and what will motivate them as individuals – this relates to finding meaning and purpose
- As a team leader, you must facilitate the process by which your

team can come up with a meaningful Success Recipe of their own. Yours, or the way yours is currently put together, may not enable your team to connect, and you will continue to bang your head against a brick wall
- Make sure that every employee is feeling validated and affirmed in a way that is meaningful to them. Don't pay attention only to big things that they do (this is what they are probably being paid to do anyway); notice the small things too – it shows that you care
- Get to know each member of your team and what makes them tick
- Find ways to help them feel more in control
- Encourage them to use curiosity instead of fear as a source of energy that fuels their work

Takeaways for winning at home and life

- It is crucial to realise how important validation is to people
    - When something you have been working hard on goes well, or you experience some kind of success, make a point of taking a moment to acknowledge your achievement
    - I have taken to ringing my own bell – literally: I keep an antique brass bell on my desk, and I ring it to acknowledge big and small successes in my day. The sound of the bell is multisensory; it anchors the acknowledgement in my whole being
- Every day, both adults and children subconsciously and non-verbally ask three questions of each other in a family:
    - Do you see me?
    - Do you hear me?
    - Am I important to you?
- If we get a 'yes' in answer to every one of these three questions, our emotional cups are filled. If not, you can be sure that negative attention-seeking behaviour will begin. We all have negative attention-seeking strategies that kick in when we are feeling short of attention. Here are some adult behaviours that you may be aware of in yourself or others in your household:
    - picking fights

  - overworking
  - sulking
  - ignoring
  - dressing up or undressing
  - affairs
  - cooking for or refusing to cook for our partners
- When children feel invisible to their parents, they also employ a wide range of attention-seeking behaviours:
  - they cry
  - they become loud and/or cheeky
  - they throw tantrums
  - they stop eating
  - they overeat
  - they refuse to sleep, or sleep all day
  - they withdraw or become clingy
  - they become ill
  - little ones regress with their toilet training
  - they ignore you (you are dead meat!)
  - they embarrass you in public
  - they show bad sportsmanship.
- It is very important to validate each other at home

Chapter 25

Positional versus personal power

Parents wield a lot of power over their children's lives. Managers wield power over their teams. Educators wield power in the classroom. In this book I have said that I regard parenting at home and leading at work as closely aligned. We are the common denominator in both teams; we influence the 'weather' and set the emotional temperature wherever we go.

We all have two kinds of power at our disposal: positional power and personal power. The use of these can have quite different results, as illustrated in this powerful statement by psychologist, educator and author Haim Ginnot:

> I've come to a frightening conclusion that I am the decisive element in the classroom. It's my personal approach that creates the climate. It's my daily mood that makes the weather. As a teacher, I possess a tremendous power to make a child's life miserable or joyous. I can be a tool of torture or an instrument of inspiration. I can humiliate or heal. In all situations, it is my response that decides whether a crisis will be escalated or de-escalated and a child humanized or dehumanized. [33]

Positional power is the 'because-I-said-so' variety. This is the power we hold because we are the parent or the boss. It is power that is generally enforceable, as it relies on our authority. Some children or team members might resist or challenge this type of power, causing conflict in the parent–child or employer–employee relationship. Has your child ever said, 'You can't make me'? Then you know what I'm talking about. I'm sure you have also experienced a chilly reception when you try to make members of your team do things versus influencing them by connecting with what they value and what makes work meaningful to them.

Personal power, by contrast, relies on our communication ability and power to influence. It used to be seen as a soft skill, but is now highly sought after because it garners respect, creates confidence and allows following based on trust. We all exercise our personal power differently because we are unique individuals. I have seen extremely quiet and gentle people wield enormous influence by using their personal power effectively, just as I have seen charismatic, 'out there' leaders do the same. In a corporate environment, managers often use positional power to ensure that things get done, while leaders are experts at using their personal power to influence and inspire people into action. Leading through personal power means giving clear guidelines, expectations and calls to action, and then letting people get on with it and take responsibility for their choices and actions.

In the home setting, one of your very important roles is to teach your children how to make their own choices and bear the consequences of these. It is wise to bear in mind the fast-changing world we live in when allowing consequences to be your child's teacher: it will not be an easy ride for anyone, so neither a completely authoritarian parenting approach nor wrapping kids in cotton wool and smoothing their path for them will cut it. At work, this approach should lead individuals to make the best choices for themselves while also supporting the Success Journey of the team.

HELPING CHILDREN MAKE GOOD CHOICES

'What do you choose?' is a question that psychologist Dr Garry Landreth, father of child-centred play therapy at the University of North Texas, believes parents should be asking their children more and more often. In his evergreen presentation 'Choices, Cookies and Kids: A Creative Approach to Discipline', he recommends that parents start offering their children choices from around the age of two years. Although this may sound early, he comments:

> When will children learn what it feels like to make a choice if we are constantly telling them what to do? Give big choices to big kids and little choices to little kids. The basis of this approach is to give two choices that both have an outcome that you are fine with. This allows you to remain in control while allowing the child to experience having control over their choice.

Here are a few examples of how to give children choices to help them practise taking responsibility for their actions – something that is vitally important as we move into an era of disruption, where self-leadership will become more important than ever.

Example 1

A four-year-old walks out of the kitchen clutching an armful of chocolate biscuits just before bedtime. Your response could be: 'You choose one and put the rest back, or you choose to put them all back. Which do you choose?' Either way, both choices should provide for an outcome you are fine with.

Example 2

'If you choose to fight in the car, then you choose not to enjoy an hour of gaming when we get home. If you choose to get along with each other, then you choose to get to game. What do you choose?'

Example 3

A seven-year-old leaves his bath towel on the floor and you respond with, 'If you choose to hang your towel up, you choose to watch your favourite TV programme tonight. If you choose not to, then you choose to stay in your room and not watch TV. What do you choose?'

A vital part of giving your children choices is that you follow through with the consequence of their choice or action. Dr Landreth stresses that in the instant a child makes a choice, such as walking past the bath towel that he left on the passage floor instead of hanging it up in the bathroom as discussed, then he has demonstrated his choice and must suffer the consequence of not watching his favourite TV programme. It's no use giving your children choices and then reminding them three times that they have forgotten to hang up the towel. This creates a nagging parent, not an empowered child. Are you a micromanager at work too? When things are feeling out of control, it's easy for leaders and managers to default to micromanaging.

By allowing children to take responsibility for their actions, they learn that you are serious about the choices you are offering and they will manipulate you less. You are also teaching your children that when they make a choice, they are committed at the very moment they choose. 'This is an invaluable life skill which may well save her life in her teenage years when she may be offered a ... recreational drug at a rave, a spiked drink in a night club, or a lift with a driver who is under the influence of alcohol,' says Dr Landreth.

You should not offer your children choices about everything in life, but rather in situations or around issues where you are trying to 'train' them to demonstrate appropriate behaviour. Some more examples:

- putting dirty clothes in the laundry basket
- taking their dirty lunchboxes from their school bag
- keeping their bedroom tidy
- tidying up toys and packing away after playing
- finishing homework before gaming or watching TV
- eating/finishing dinner
- going to bed at the right time.

'Don't overdose on giving choices, as they are much like Aspirin,' quips Dr Landreth. 'Two will generally clear a headache and a hundred in a day will kill you!'

There is a time and place for both types of power in parent–child relationships and employer–employee relationships. Positional power translates to authority and personal power to leadership.

If you repeatedly find yourself saying, 'Because I said so!' to establish yourself as the boss, then it may be time to start using more personal than positional power in your parenting or management approach. The more inspirational you are, the less energy you will expend having to convince your children or your team that you are actually in charge. I, for one, am into conserving as much of my energy as possible!

INFLUENCING YOUR TEAM MEMBERS TO MAKE CHOICES THAT SUPPORT THE TEAM

In my work with teams, the most common feedback from team members about what weakens the team is not having an idea of the big picture. This makes them feel as though they are operating in a vacuum with no clear purpose. Whatever your goal is for your team, it's no good if they don't buy into it. Therefore, you will need to be open-minded and embark on an unpacking and repackaging process with your team so that they collaborate and co-create the Success Journey together with you, and buy into the vision they create around the challenge that you have given them. In essence, they collaboratively create a story that is meaningful to them, that will hold their attention and galvanise their effort.

When they see how their contribution to the big picture can help them to successfully meet their key performance indicators and at the same time build their own talent profile, they will want to be involved and your team will be energised. What creates value and meaning for one team member will not be the same for another. This is Happy Juice in action (see Chapter 24).

As a team leader you have to be seen to be giving your own energy leadership, keeping the team in the loop and acknowledging progress. If you have taken time to get to know your team members individually, you will be able to customise your feedback in ways that connect with what is meaningful to that person. This will get team members on your side.

Make sure that everyone knows their roles and responsibilities. Assume nothing. Ask for feedback to find out if they do. Ensure that everyone takes responsibility for their role in the bigger story and for their own commitments. Assign tasks to the right person in the team. Holacracy is the approach of giving tasks to the person most skilled to do the job, regardless of how senior or junior they are in the team. This more modern approach will lead to having a flexible and nimble team that plays to the strengths of the group.

Be decisive but flexible. Always be open to new ways of doing things by being approachable and supportive. Set an example of willingness to learn and that you are bold enough to disrupt yourself. Just because things have always been done one way doesn't mean that they should stay that way. You want a team that thinks robustly and challenges the status quo. However, just as a parent is not a 'peerent' (their child's friend), you do not have to be friends with your team. But you do need to listen. Your openness, integrity, consistency and basic humanity will go a long way towards building a culture of belonging and togetherness – that sense of family that we all seek – that will make people stay or recommend you when they leave, possibly making them boomerang to join you again sometime in the future.

Takeaways for winning at work

- We use both personal and positional power at work
- Too often we abuse power – consciously or unconsciously exerting power over each other or power against one another
  - You can't make anyone do anything by force without them resenting you; you can try by commanding and demanding, but it's not sustainable and the effect won't last
- Use the power of influence to bring improvement and momentum to your team
- Influence is underpinned by trust and confidence in the leader, so answer these two questions honestly:
  - Are you trustworthy?
  - Do you inspire confidence?
- Lead by example
- Praise outcomes
- Encourage the process of working towards a goal
- Praise strategy and effort
- Exhibit patience and kindness
- Be firm
- Provide boundaries – they help team members to feel safe

Takeaways for winning at home and life

- Be clear and firm yet loving with your family
- Influence your children to be their best selves
- Lead by example – children will do what you *do* and not what you say – you are role-modelling either constructive or destructive use of personal and positional power
- As your children grow older, give them the power of choice
- Always follow through with the consequence of your child's choice
- Don't get emotional when they make a poor choice
  - Stay calm
  - 'I see you've chosen not to hang up your towel, so you have chosen not to watch TV, so off you go and read a book'
  - They are imposing the choice – not you

    - If they get upset, calmly say, 'Next time you can choose differently'
- Don't be the nagging parent – you don't want them to need micromanaging at work one day
- Raise children who take responsibility for their choices and accept the consequences
- Rather let them learn this at an early age, when the consequences of poor choices have less of an impact than not completing a portfolio piece when they are in matric

Chapter 26

Self-discovery through parenting

It is my fundamental belief that parenting is one of the most incredible personal development adventures you will ever have. It's a disruptive journey for sure: there is much you cannot anticipate or control that will require a creative and conscious response in the moment. And it is very personal, because you will discover more about who you are along the way.

Our children have a 360-degree view of us, thus helping us to discover parts of us we never knew existed had we not become a parent. They are continually bringing those discoveries to us and non-verbally inviting us to dance – with ourselves. It is up to us whether we say yes or no, and whether we are prepared to engage and grow, or not. Parenting is not only about raising our children, it is about being prepared to raise ourselves and become more conscious of who we are in the process.

If you can see parenting in this way, it becomes less of a to-do list and more about a state of being. This makes parenting worth all the effort, time and energy it requires. You should not be left an empty shell at the end of it all, but rather more of who you are – 'bigger' than you were before you became a parent.

Family is your child's first team. Within the 'we', they discover the 'me'. This is very important from a role-modelling perspective because children learn what they see. They take in more cues from what you *do* than from what you say. This means being as congruent as possible with our words and actions. What many parents miss, however, is that their family is also *their* team.

In *The Conscious Parent*, a *New York Times* bestseller by Shefali Tsabary, I found a passage that echoes my sentiments but in completely different words. I want to share it with you:

> While we believe we hold the power to raise our children, the reality is that our children hold the power to raise *us* into the parents they need us to become. For this reason, the parenting experience isn't one of the parent *versus* the child but of the parent *with* the child. The road to wholeness sits in our children's lap, and all we need to do is take a seat. As our children show us our way back to our own essence, they become our greatest awakeners. If we fail to hold their hand and follow their lead as they usher us through the gateway of increased consciousness, we lose the chance to walk toward our own enlightenment.

Shefali goes on to say:

> When I speak of our children transforming us as parents, don't for a moment imagine I'm advocating relinquishing our influence on our children and becoming their minions. As much as conscious parenting is about listening to our children, honouring their essence, and being fully present with them, it is also about boundaries and discipline. As parents, we are required to provide our children not only with the basics of shelter, food and education, but also to teach them the value of structure, appropriate containment of their emotions, and such skills as reality testing. In other words, conscious parenting encompasses all aspects of bringing up a child to be a well-rounded, balanced member of the human race. Hence there is nothing *permissive* about parenting consciously.[34]

My wish for you is that you are able to engage in the dance of connection with your children on this incredible personal development adventure we all embark on – that of raising each other up. Parenting holds multiple lessons and opportunities for future-proofing yourself and your children in the process. It provides a great training ground for managing your team at work. If you have issues in both your home and your work teams, remember that you are the common denominator. Working on yourself can lead to instant changes in both camps – the ripple effect can be very powerful. Take this saying to heart: When you point one finger at someone else, there are three fingers pointing back at you.

FIX YOURSELF, FIX YOUR CHILD

Many years ago, when my husband and I went through a rough patch, as relationships do from time to time, our communication wasn't great. We were withholding many of our pent-up thoughts and feelings from each other and this was manifesting itself in the behaviour of our then three-year-old son. Fortunately, I figured out that his behaviour was connected to our lack of communication and that if we got clear with each other, then there would be no reason to have to 'fix' our child.

So I put my theory on the table. My husband and I agreed to get clear with each other right there and then, and it was remarkable to see that within just a few minutes (yes, I said minutes) of mom and dad sorting out their issues – getting over themselves – the negative behaviour pattern in our boy had disappeared, completely.

It really was one of those 'aha' parenting moments for us, because our choice in that instant yielded an immediate positive outcome – proof that our children are more perceptive than we give them credit for. They are deeply connected to us, after all. They know us well: all our strengths, weaknesses, the subtle nuances in our characters and whether things are going well or not. We don't even have to verbalise any of this, they know it or sense it.

We also forget that our children are watching us, copying us and tapping into who we are. We are their role models. How they see us acting or reacting to life on a daily basis will form their values and world view, as well as their attitudes towards other people, work, learning and challenges. You might be grappling with work pressure, financial issues or a stressful relationship. They are witnesses to it all. But change the way you do things, or change your attitude towards them, and it is remarkable how you can, in many instances, turn negative experiences and situations into positive teachable moments that can serve your children well in their future, even if they were traumatic at the time.

Sometimes the quickest way to deal with issues in your child is to look first to see where or how they are reflecting you. The moment you accept that you are a contributor to what you are seeing in your child, you will find yourself in a powerful position to change the song you are singing, lifting the burden from your child that she has perhaps innocently and unwittingly taken on, allowing her to shine again.

The father of analytical psychology, Carl Jung, said in 1939 that if there is anything we wish to change in a child, we should examine whether it is something that could be better changed in ourselves. Jung's words closely parallel Gandhi's now famous words, 'Be the change you want to see in the world.' More often than not, it starts with you, in your home team and in your work team.

Takeaways for winning at work

- Fix yourself, fix your team
  - Look for patterns of behaviour; they are useful pointers
  - Are you experiencing similar issues at work and at home?
  - You may be the common denominator and that's where the change needs to happen
- Don't for a minute think that stresses at work don't go home with you
- All stresses are opportunities for learning and growth

Takeaways for winning at home and life

- Don't play the 'name, blame and shame' game
- When you point a finger at someone else, always remember that three fingers are pointing back at you
- Take responsibility for your own attitude and behaviour
- Children are more perceptive than you think
- Children will try to fix you if they sense there is a problem
  - Be clear that you created the problem, not them, and that you have to fix it; it's not their problem to solve
- If you are in a relationship:
  - Strive for honest communication
  - Don't hold on to issues – undelivered communication becomes toxic to your relationship
  - Create a safe space where you can be honest with each other. This needs to be a check-in process during which you put your thoughts and feelings on the table so that the other person knows

where you are coming from, they understand your point of view and really hear you

- This check-in process could relate to your relationship or the events of the day (pick one)
- Give each other the opportunity to say:
  - This is what is working for me…
  - This is what is not working for me…
  - Do this on a regular basis without trying to fix each other or demand remedial action, and see what happens
  - Honesty and really listening can often trump the need to use power over each other
  - As your children get older, you can engage in the above check-in process with them to foster honest communication in a safe space

Chapter 27

It's all your time

In her book *Parenting with Spirit*, Jane Bartlett quotes exiled Vietnamese Zen master and peace activist Thich Nhat Hanh, who wrote about a father of two who decides not to divide his time into parts any more. This father tries to consider the time he spends helping his wife, or helping his sons with homework, as his own time too. His own time (not work time) is no longer about going for nice walks by himself or reading a book: his own time is *everything* he does. So he finds ways of enjoying his family's presence and fully engaging with them. 'The remarkable thing is that now I have unlimited time for myself!' he says.

If we can see parenting as part of *our* life's journey and not merely another thing on our to-do list each day, then we have the privilege of taking part in the most wonderful adventure of personal discovery that will leave us larger than we were before. But we must acknowledge that we will need to be present to take advantage of the opportunity that lies ahead, and we must learn how to look at our allocation of time differently.

Try to be emotionally present in what you are doing, especially when you are with your children. Try to savour what you are doing. Enjoy the world from a child's perspective: children's sense of wonder and fascination for life is infectious. Recognise when you are feeling off-balance and need to restore yourself. Explore how your experience of time changes when you don't divide it up rigidly into time for others and 'me time'. See it all as time for yourself, and you will have time for what matters most.

AIM FOR DYNAMIC BALANCE

It is time to rid your mind of any notions of Supermom or Superdad. Once in a blue moon you will hit the jackpot and a day will pan out exactly as you had planned, but mostly it won't. Think about a see-saw in a playground: when it's moving, it's in dynamic balance; when it gets stuck up or down, it's not. We need to aim for dynamic balance, not perfect balance. That's work–life integration. Most parents heave a sigh of relief when I tell them this.

Let's aim for workable solutions instead of perfect ones. Let's learn to be more emotionally present instead of showering our children with gifts to compensate for our absence. We need to remind ourselves that we are dealing with human beings. In our quest for an organised life, let's avoid falling into the trap of micromanaging our families like human resources. They are people who need boundaries as much as they need our time, our presence and our love.

Takeaways for winning at work

- Treat your team at work like you would family
- Listen to them
- Care for them – it's a massive motivator in the workplace
- Put the human in the middle
- Show empathy for people's situations and circumstances without rescuing them
- Be interested in their journey with their family
- Know how many children they have and all the relevant details so that you can ask questions that show you are paying attention and that you care

Takeaways for winning at home and life

- Being a parent is part of who you are, not only what you do
- Your time spent parenting is your primary leadership role
- Spot the leadership lessons you develop at home that could work in business
- See yourself as a whole person
- Consider your family as a team
- Engage in deep listening at home so that you get to know each other and each other's hopes and dreams
- It's as important to know what motivates your family members as it is to know what motivates your team members at work

Chapter 28

Future-proof your child

In my 'Let Go & Let Grow' parenting talk[35] on raising independent, resilient children, I describe the Burj Al Arab, the beautiful sail-shaped hotel on a man-made island off the coast of Dubai. It is underpinned by 230 concrete piles that reach 40 metres deep and are 1.5 metres wide, and it took five years to build – three of which were spent on building the foundations alone. That in itself is a lesson in parenting – our children need wide and deep foundations on which to one day create their own life of meaning independent of ours. These foundations, I believe, are less influenced by school than you think. *You* are the hidden curriculum, and you have an incredibly powerful impact on your child or children and on how prepared they are for the future.

In this chapter, I share the five building blocks Graeme Codrington and I developed in our book *Future-proof Your Child for the 2020s and Beyond.*

FIVE BUILDING BLOCKS TO FUTURE-PROOF YOUR CHILD

While no one can be fully future-proof, as a parent you need the peace of mind that you have done all you can to prepare your children for a world of multiple disruptions so that they can harness the winds and tides of change. Of course, you are not the only influence. Other adults, children, institutions and life experiences will shape your children too. But you can use these five building blocks as a guide on your parenting journey.

Family

Family is where all future-proofing begins – within the 'we' your children discover the 'me'. No matter the size, shape or gender of your family, family is where hope lives. It's where patterns for learning, relationships and values are laid.

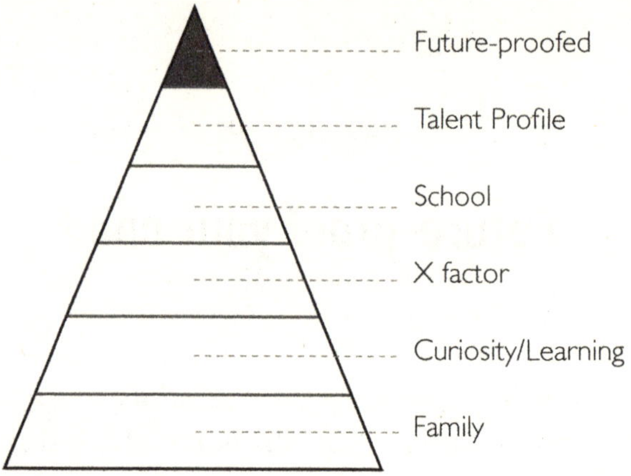

Figure 2: The building blocks to future-proof your child

Curiosity and learning

Curiosity and learning come next. Children are naturally curious. We don't need to teach them how to learn – they are wired for learning. Our job is to keep their curiosity for learning alive. One of the clear and present dangers in the current-crisis schooling model is that children are either overstimulated, overwhelmed, or under-stimulated and losing their love of learning.

X factors for success

Children catch X factors for success primarily via osmosis – from watching their parents or significant adults rather than by learning them from a book. In other words, they are caught and not taught. They are difficult to measure or test, but they are more essential than ever. What I am talking about here are attributes that future employers will be looking out for in their employees (see also Chapter 20, where I unpack these in more detail):

- Curiosity
- A love for learning
- Resilience
- Self-knowledge
- Ability to relate to others (being part of a team).

School

School is a place where students follow a formal curriculum, where they learn in groups, and where they are tested and assessed on a regular basis against a standard set of norms. The nature of school and education will be undergoing rapid transformation in the next few years. The global pandemic has accelerated this shift. Watch this space, as parents and children will have increasing choice in how to do school.

Talent profile

Helping your children to turn their X factors for success into a multimedia talent profile, which is far more than a conventional CV, will prepare them for finding a good match between their skills, qualifications and interests, and the world of work. Help them on their journey to discover the essence of who they are – the gifts they bring to the world beyond being athletic, mathematical, linguistic or artistic. Read more about the contents of a talent profile in Chapter 20.

If you focus on putting these five building blocks in place with your child, you will have peace of mind that you have done the best you can to future-proof them so that they can leave you, live independently of you, and go out and create their own version of happiness and success. At the rate the world is changing, their version of happiness and success is likely to be very different from the picture you have in your head.

This means that you need to be open-minded and flexible, and be open to expanding your view of talent beyond your offspring's athletic or academic abilities. Help your child to discover the essence of who they are – and don't underestimate your role in helping them move along on this journey. Family is where hope lives!

Takeaways for winning at work

- Overlay the five building blocks for future-proofing your child on your team at work
    - The bottom layer of family in this instance is your work team
    - Encourage curiosity about what you can do and learn together

- Support the development of X factors at and through work
- Upskill and reskill at work
- Each member of the team creates their own talent profile instead of a conventional CV

Takeaways for winning at home and life

- Family is where hope lives
- Build broad, deep emotional foundations in your kids so that they can withstand the winds and tides of change
- Help every member of the family create their talent profile from eight years and up
- Create an awareness of the importance of X factors for success instead of merely looking at academic marks
- Keep your own talent profile up to date and at the ready for peace of mind

Chapter 29

Leading from the inside out

Let's not get stuck thinking that the only real leaders in society are those who are publicly visible – such as CEOs of large organisations, politicians or social activists – or that they are only the head boys or head girls or team captains at school. Some children are natural-born leaders from the start, and remain so for the rest of their lives. These children are few and far between. They have charisma, magnetism, confidence, principles and opinions. But most children develop their leadership ability over time, and gradually come into their own in very interesting ways. I am, in fact, a fan of late bloomers!

As they become more sure of who they are, they are able to express their leadership ability in both small and large ways, and in private as well as public arenas. We need to encourage our children to first and foremost practise and develop the art of effective personal leadership on a daily basis – long before they ever have the opportunity to hold any kind of official public leadership position.

In this chapter I provide a checklist for developing the building blocks for personal leadership. All the points in this list are equally applicable to adults and to developing children, namely:

- Taking responsibility for your actions and controlling your reactions
- Looking after your property and belongings
- Developing and expressing your opinions
- Communicating clearly with others
- Developing self-discipline
- Learning to work within boundaries and being creative within limits
- Learning when it's okay to break the rules
- Letting go of assumptions and being willing to be wrong

- Learning that leaders don't always follow the crowd and being okay with that
- Learning not to be swayed by the crowd unless it is in line with your principles
- Learning how to evaluate situations and think critically
- Asking good questions and really listening to the answers
- Taking positive and negative feedback and using it constructively
- Understanding what triggers you to react and how to manage that
- Developing empathy for others
- Being prepared to get one's hands dirty in the trenches
- Stepping back from time to time to keep perspective
- Developing a problem-solving mentality
- Earning a reputation for delivering on what you promise – for keeping your word
- Being an example of someone embracing the future and preparing for it
- Being prepared to experiment and fail.

There is, of course, much more to leadership than can be covered by a checklist, but if we can help our children master some or all of the above, they will have made huge strides towards leading themselves from the inside out. This, in turn, will enable them to lead in their own sphere of influence when the time is right. Encourage your children continually to learn the art of leading from the inside out. It's a skill that will serve them well forever, especially in disruptive times, as they will have to lead themselves through much turbulence and mist.

Takeaways for winning at work

- Leading and managing yourself is life leadership; self-leadership has never been more important than now
- Leadership is not about naming, shaming and blaming, but about raising yourself and others up
- Leadership is taking personal responsibility for every choice you make in life and owning your part in every situation that goes right and wrong

- You cannot make others do anything; you can only influence them with your personal or positional power

Takeaways for winning at home and life

- Parenting is primary leadership
- You can lead from the front, from the back and from the side – parents need to do all three at different times
- You are a role model for your child
- Children take their cues from what you do rather than from what you say, so your actions need to match your words
- Encourage your children to take responsibility for their choices from an early age – it is an empowering life skill
- Don't always solve your children's problems for them immediately or provide them with solutions
- Ask children what they think or what they think they should do instead of rescuing them
- Help your children to learn to cope with criticism
- You want children who believe 'I am, I can and I will' – this is self-leadership in action

Chapter 30

Shepherd your energy

One dark winter's morning I was up early to beat the rush-hour traffic for a presentation to the partners and senior partners of a large international accounting and consulting firm (this was pre-pandemic and after my husband's death). I remember looking at my bed and thinking, 'No one will know if I don't make my bed this morning. My sons are away, and my domestic helper doesn't work today. Is it really important to make my bed?'

A small voice inside me answered, 'Leadership is all about how we get up, show up, and shepherd our own energy and the energy of others. We have to choose to bring order to chaos, to give our energy direction. Making your bed is a very tangible, concrete example of bringing order to chaos, and choosing the direction of the energy.' So I made my bed, and in doing so I created a great opening story for a company and an industry that was in complete turmoil at that time.

As I drove to my destination, it also occurred to me, not for the first time, that I had the privilege of the platform. That morning I was being given the leadership mantle by the partners and senior partners of a major company and I needed to shepherd my own energy so that I could bring order to theirs. That is self-leadership, and it has a ripple effect on everyone in our home team and our work team without us having to say a word.

We have all been knocked by the pandemic, and some have been knocked down by What If™ moments in life and by Covid-19. Our self-confidence may have been dented or shattered, leaving us feeling out of control. Learning to get up and dust ourselves off is about grit, determination and perseverance. Every time we commit to moving forward, even in small ways, we grow our resilience muscle. Learning something new takes practice and perseverance. Being in a new space takes adjustment. We are making a transition, and that requires many choices and actions along the way to avoid getting stuck in hopelessness and helplessness. We need to develop grit to have hope.

Angela Duckworth, author of *Grit: The Power of Passion and Perseverance,* aptly states:

> One kind of hope is the expectation that tomorrow will be better than today. It's the kind of hope that has us yearning for sunnier weather, or a smoother path ahead. It comes without the burden of responsibility. The onus is on the universe to make things better.
>
> Grit depends on a different kind of hope. It rests on the expectation that our own efforts can improve our future. *I have a feeling tomorrow will be better* is different from *I resolve to make tomorrow better.* The hope that gritty people have has nothing to do with luck and everything to do with getting up again.[36]

In these times of uncertainty, I encourage you to ask yourself every morning, 'How might today surprise me?' And every evening before you go to bed, ask yourself, 'How did today surprise me?' When you are going through a disruptive time, this is a wonderful way to keep an open mind to newness, possibility and opportunity.

Self-leadership in changing times demands that we begin from a place of not knowing and having no right answers. You've never been here before. You will figure it out and *feel your way* towards what's right for you. Acceptance will move you forward. Anger will keep you stuck in the past. Don't look back!

Takeaways for winning at work

- You do not have to be the boss to be an energy shepherd; each one of us is responsible for how we direct our energy every moment of every day
- Our energy and our choices are inextricably intertwined
- Even if you don't consciously choose to direct your energy, that in itself is a choice
- Can you think of examples of when your choice about how to direct your energy had a direct impact on your team?

- Beware of energy vampires – people who suck you dry; spend as little time as possible with them
- Become aware of people who boost your energy; spend more time with them
- Look at how different jobs you have had have provided you with the opportunity to give your energy leadership and direction in different ways

Takeaways for winning at home and life

- Parents are like the weather: you determine the emotional temperature in your home, so be aware of your impact on your family and how reactive you are being
- Every thought or free choice you make and every behaviour or action you take is based on love or fear
    - Fear contracts, it closes us down, wrapping us tightly in its clutches
    - Love opens us up, gives itself away, holds us close and then lets us go
    - Are you allowing love or fear to direct your energy?
- Claim your space, claim your time, claim your energy
    - This is tough to do when your children are very young (read Chapter 7 for more on managing your time with children) because a lot of your time and energy will be directed at doing what needs to be done with and for your children
    - It is essential to reframe how you see your time in this season of your life to avoid frustration
    - Who are you choosing to spend time with and how does that affect how you direct your energy? Some people energise us and others can suck us dry. Some people have a healthy influence on us and others distract us from doing what is good for us. Become more discerning as to who you choose to spend your time with

SELF-REFLECTION REVISITED

Exercise 1: Let's test your emotional temperature right now

If you have read the whole book, then it's time to test your emotional temperature again. I do this exercise for a second time at the end of my 'Reframing Disruption to Win @ Work and Life' presentations too. So do this exercise again to ascertain how you are feeling *right now* after reading this book.

Which statement most accurately reflects how you feel?

- Fearful and depressed
- Anxious and overwhelmed
- Reasonably in control
- Coping and confident
- Positive and optimistic about the future

Which statement did you circle when you started reading this book? Which statement have you circled now? Did it show a positive shift in your thoughts and feelings in dealing with the disruption you are currently facing? This shift, experienced by all my audiences when they redo this exercise, illustrates the power of reframing.

Exercise 2: Where is your thinking?

I encourage you to repeat Caspar Craven's exercise again too. Where is your thinking now? Has it shifted?

PAST		PRESENT		FUTURE	

Are you less focused on the past now than at the beginning of this book? There is no perfect ratio for past, present, future thinking – it is what it is. Just remember that it certainly gives you a good idea of how much energy you expend on being in the past, in the present or in the future. This might explain why your perspective on the world could be very different from someone else's.

If you are struggling, don't despair. Everyone may become overwhelmed by life, even in non-pandemic times. We can get stuck in the past, thinking about what has happened, what didn't work out, or how we want to go back to a better time. We can be paralysed by our fear of an unknown future and project feelings of lack of agency and control. In both situations, we forget about the power of the present moment. This is where our control and personal power lie. So take things moment by moment, and be mindful that what you do today counts. The choices you make today determine the picture on your canvas, and tomorrow there will be a new canvas! Nobody can go back and make a new beginning, but anyone can start today and make a new ending. I encourage you to hold on to that thought and the possibilities that are within your reach – every day.

CONCLUSION

There is an ebb and flow in life, a giving and a taking, many endings and new beginnings. No one's life unfolds in a straight line. There are life tremors, small warnings, and then there are life quakes with the capacity to throw us off-centre completely.

What did you find when the mist started to lift, or when you opened the door in your moment of disruption? Your journey with change of any kind will be as unique as you are, and no change or loss is any more or less profound than that of any other person. So don't judge, but rather choose to dance with it.

Whether you lose your health, wealth, marriage, job, business, your family through emigration or your personal freedom, you will go through the very same process of adjustment and transition as someone who loses a special person to crime, illness or in a horrific car accident. Remember that you will go through the same process too when it comes to positive changes that you choose in life, such as moving town, country, jobs, schools and into new relationships – for all the right reasons!

When human beings experience change, they are deprived of what is familiar and comfortable, and it takes time and effort to move through this phase of uncertainty. Even the coronavirus – that global teachable 'moment' that has affected us all in different ways – has set us on that same trajectory.

Whatever adjustment you are dealing with, acknowledge that it is big for you. You can remain buried by it, frozen in fear, or stuck in the past, or you can choose to be broken open by it and planted like a seed. You can recover from change, or you can discover – there is a significant difference. Discovery is a process fuelled by curiosity instead of fear and wrapped in gratitude rather than bitterness and anger. You have to walk into your fear and your pain. You have to face the issues change raises for you and work through them. That is where your growth and new possibilities lie, for we are not the same person we were at the start of the journey.

Allow me to return to the lesson of where we all find ourselves: in the middle of the mists of not knowing exactly what the future looks like beyond the coronavirus pandemic, knowing that there are a host of disruptive forces and megatrends on the way, and believing that we are more wired to cope with change than we think. I hope the key messages, lessons and insights contained in this book will help you on your journey to future-proofing yourself. I challenge you to:

- Turn full stops into commas
- Understand disruption and the grief/loss connection
- Make yourself supportable instead of waiting to be rescued
- Participate in your own rescue
- Choose to be broken open and planted rather than being a victim
- Stop trying to fix broken pictures – rather create new ones
- Move beyond the past, where your personal power is at its lowest
- Design your future in anticipation instead of waiting for the future to arrive
- Prepare for a marathon, not a sprint – life is a process, not a single event
- Keep your human energy battery charged – only you can do this
- Avoid Popped Elastic Band Syndrome – get the balance between pressure and tension right

- Let your glitter settle – it always does
- Be curious instead of fearful
- Go to the bottom of the emotional well, but don't get stuck there
- Look for workable solutions – not perfect ones
- Share your humanity and vulnerability
- Stop and be quiet from time to time – listen with more than just your ears
- Make time for self-reflection; it's what successful people do
- Relinquish judgement of yourself and others – it gets in your way
- Shepherd your energy – what you focus on will flourish
- Put the human in the middle
- Connect head and heart
- Be prepared to upskill, reskill or reinvent yourself to remain relevant
- Ring your bell to affirm and validate your own progress
- See yourself as a valuable asset (remember Brand Me Inc.)
- Develop your X factors for success and package them in a talent profile
- Remember that you are one person belonging to multiple teams at home, at work and in life – they are all spaces for self-expression.

We are learning to trust that:

- We will figure it out
- We will adapt
- The world is not ending – it is changing
- If we co-create the future, we will go further.

We are human beings. Our bodies and brains are built to adapt. We are known as a complex adaptive system for a reason. We are unaware of the thousands of processes going on inside us 24/7 to keep us alive; how the human body lives on the edge of chaos so that it can adapt and respond to change from moment to moment. The ability to create order out of chaos is wired into our DNA, into our heads and our hearts, even when it hurts. Finding the balance between head and heart is part of the journey. We are emotional beings and we need to honour our emotions and yet not get overwhelmed and paralysed by them. Living only from our heads would mean showing up as only half a person.

Our bodies are creating order out of chaos even though we are not aware of it. Our heads might get on with the job, sometimes with finesse and at other times like the proverbial bull in a china shop, but our hearts – our bruised and broken hearts – take time to catch up and make sense of it all. This is why we need to have compassion and empathy for ourselves too, and not only for other people. This is easier said than done (I should know). I will never forget one of my husband's university mates sending me a message after the funeral that said, 'Be gentle with yourself.' Initially, it just made me mad. 'I don't even know what that word means any more!' was my response. How can you be gentle with yourself when your husband has just been murdered in cold blood and you feel like your country has betrayed you?

In time I have come to understand the meaning of being gentle with myself. I had to give myself time and space to grieve and process my loss so that I could truly heal. I had to hold the heat of the pain, the size of the loss, and the depth of the shift close enough to hear the whispers of the lessons, to embrace them, and give the process time without knowing when or where it would end.

This is what I wrote on Facebook in a post on 23 November 2020, just after the third anniversary of my husband's death:

*Last week was the third anniversary of Si's death. It has taken me a while to process it. Although time heals, one never knows what cellular memory is going to throw up. It always seems to catch one off-guard, and this year was no exception – proving, once again, my sister's most prophetic statement in the early stages of dealing with what happened, that this thing has more layers than a f***ing onion. Just as you peel away one layer there just seems to be another. She was so right!*

I clearly remember being told on a number of occasions in the first month or two that this trauma would take 18 months to three years to process and come to terms with. At the time that felt like a life sentence, but those who have walked this road before me, of losing a loved one to crime, were right. Time does, indeed, heal and you learn to absorb the loss into the fabric of who you are and grow with it. So, I acknowledge this three-year milestone of walking in and out of the shadowlands and out into the sunshine again.

To the many friends and family who have held the space for us and, at times, held their breath for us, you have been such an incredible support. Proof that we do not travel this life alone.

I am now sucking the marrow out of life. Each and every day is a gift. It has its own yin and yang to it. Its own dynamic balance vs perfect balance. Somewhere in between extreme happiness and success and extreme sadness and despair, I have discovered that there is a place where one can experience a deep and powerful sense of satisfaction and contentment.

It's all about the lens through which you view the world, how you work with change and disruption, who you surround yourself with, and taking responsibility for your choices and attitude in each and every moment of being alive.

Expressing gratitude for what you have instead of focusing only on what you have lost, and embracing the ambiguity of life, resonates deeply for me, and maybe for you – whatever you are going through or have gone through.

In the hundreds of pieces of poetry I have written about love, life and loss, this one in particular expresses the duality of life:

You have been broken open
You are not broken
Life has come
To teach your soul
To sing its song
Life has not come
To punish you
And break you
Your journey is
To piece it all together
Into one magnificent
Unique creation
That is yours, alone
A simple
And complicated
Expression
Of
You

The overriding message in this book is that curiosity is the antidote to fear. Anaïs Nin wrote, 'Life shrinks and expands in proportion to one's courage.' I would add curiosity to the mix, as all growth and expansion comes through a good dose of being curious about what lies beyond the mist and what might happen when you step beyond the door of your current reality.

I hope this book has given you an appreciation for who you are, the unique journey you have walked thus far, and made you realise that loss, grief and change are part of our contract with life, and that you can always, now and in the future, choose between a comma and a full stop.

To expand on Nin's words, I believe that life shrinks and expands in proportion to our courage – and our curiosity. May your curiosity be stronger than your fear.

ACKNOWLEDGEMENTS

To my publisher, Marlene Fryer, and managing editor, Ronel Richter-Herbert, at Penguin Random House, who spotted the work I was doing in the world at the start of the Covid-19 crisis: thanks to you, a white paper on the realities of working from home with kids became a book! You helped me turn my lived experience of building a business and brand from home with kids, together with my experience with disruption and loss, into something that I hope will help many more people to survive and thrive in these times of global change. To my editor, Christa Büttner-Rohwer, for your care and sensitive handling of this manuscript: I am thrilled you enjoyed it so much! And to my proofreader, Alice Inggs, for her attention to detail. Your positive feedback that you were moved, uplifted and inspired made this so worthwhile.

To my friend, Merrilee van Niekerk, who is also a psychologist and was a university friend of my husband's, for the inspiration of the Comma Full Stop analogy on the night of Si's funeral: it became my framework for getting up again and moving forward with my life. Merrils, thank you for tasking me with turning a full stop into a comma and for reminding me that the responsibility for creating the dots in my life was mine alone. Through my presentations and my writing, the Comma Full Stop© framework has become and remains at the core of my work. It was your gift to me, and through my work it is a gift that keeps on giving to many.

To those who have shared their insights on grief and loss with me, thank you. Particularly Dave de Vos, army mate and golfing partner to Si, and a superb cheerleader to me in grief: thank you for your encouragement and insights on this journey that you know all too well. You helped me understand that I was not losing it and that I would find a parking place and a purpose for my pain. Through you I was able to embrace the duality of loss.

Although in this book I cherry-pick only small bits from the full, messy and complicated story of my husband's murder and its aftermath, I owe an enormous debt of gratitude to my immediate family and large circle of friends. Without your incredible love, patience and support I would not be living the rich, colourful life I am able to experience today. You don't realise how kind the world really is until you experience unspeakable trauma. Maybe one day I will be brave enough to write the full account of what happened and then I will be able to mention and thank many of you by name.

Finding my voice against the backdrop of trauma and loss, especially because my work (and my life) is so very public, was daunting at times. To my very dear friend Margie Peel, for accompanying me to my first presentation after losing my husband, for literally walking and talking me back onto the stage again, and for believing in me and willing me back on my feet.

To my colleagues in the speaking community, locally and internationally, thank you for your support – in particular to the Professional Speakers Association of Southern Africa (PSASA). To Jacques Velleman, fellow speaker and friend, and lover of great books: thank you for your insight and support; your gift of Elizabeth Lesser's book *Broken Open* was a turning point on my journey.

To Douglas Kruger, colleague, friend, fellow inductee in the Speaker Hall of Fame, consummate award-winning speaker and multiple bestselling business and personal finance author, thank you for helping me craft my first 'Six Minutes That Changed My Life' presentation when I could barely remember the day of the week or my own name! You helped me to cut through the overwhelm to discover my core message – and that it is powerful and worth sharing.

To Juliette Jenner, soul sister and performance coach who just gets me: you helped me to access the voice of the mage (wise one), the speaker and the teacher rather than the widow amid the spiralling vortex of PTSD and attendant ADD in the first year of my bereavement. Thank you for speaking soul language to me, enabling me to cut through the noise in my head, to find the heartbeat beneath my words, encouraging me to connect with my audiences from a space of vulnerability, and learning how to lead with love, grace and a new sense purpose. Through your special magic, in just one short hour, you helped me to reconnect head, heart and body so that I could trust myself to share this story.

To my clients who encouraged me to share aspects of my story with their audiences from the stage, and now in webinars: thank you for trusting me to use my insights to inspire and help you move forward. These experiences have contributed enormously to the growth of my body of work in raising human potential, and of parenting both ourselves and our children, which extends way beyond this book. From individuals who have been broken open by change and loss to helping people prepare for a loss of any kind in the future, to those who provide services to traumatised clients in the legal to financial services sectors and much more, it has been a privilege to work with you all and to share my journey.

To the many counsellors, coaches and therapists who have assisted me (and continue to do so) in peeling away the many layers of the onion that is grief so that I could make sense of my situation, grow from it and move forward: the work you do in the world is invaluable as you help your clients to integrate what goes on in their lives.

To the cheerleaders in my business team who help me to show up professionally every day – Carmen Peters, Alison Ritchie and Ryan Bush. You support me not only practically, but have all lived through your own 'what if' moments, which have made you empathetic to the human condition and able to support my vision.

To Buster Sefor: you have been such an unexpected surprise on my life journey. Thank you for regularly allowing me to drench your shoulders with my tears, for just holding me and for not trying to fix me. Your patience, generosity, kindness and lifetime commitment to creating a world that works for everyone have helped me to see myself differently on this path of reinvention through disruption. Your support of and belief in me during the writing process, when I was tired and doubting myself and my message, has been a tremendous gift.

To my precious sons, Ryan and Matthew: you may both be in your twenties, but you still give me a reason to get up every day, to work on myself and be the best version of me I can be. Even though it hasn't been easy, you have both taught me so much as we worked through the biggest disruption of our lives each in our different ways.

Last but not least: thank you, dear reader. I hope that this book inspires and supports you on your life journey, wherever it takes you. Remember that you are not alone, that change is part of what makes us human, and that you are more wired for dealing with change than you think. You can learn, grow, heal, and become more than you were before despite what life throws at you or what it takes from you.

With much love and belief in you,
Nikki

RECOMMENDED READING

Bartlett, Jane. *Parenting with Spirit: 30 Ways to Nurture Your Child's Spirituality and Enrich Your Family's Life*, Boston: Da Capo Lifelong Books, 2004.

Britton, Dan, Jimmy Page and Jon Gordon. *One Word That Will Change Your Life*, Hoboken: Wiley, 2013.

Brown, Brené. *Daring Greatly: How the Courage to Be Vulnerable Transforms the Way We Live, Love, Parent, and Lead*, New York: Avery, 2015.

Buckingham, Marcus. *Find Your Strongest Life: What the Happiest and Most Successful Women Do Differently*, Nashville: One Thing Productions, 2009.

Bush, Nikki and Graeme Codrington. *Future-proof Your Child for the 2020s and Beyond*, Cape Town: Penguin Random House, 2019.

Cameron, Julia. *The Artist's Way*, London: Pan Books, 1994.

Campbell, Joseph. *The Power of Myth*, New York: Doubleday, 1998.

Craven, Caspar. *Be more Human: Rethinking the Rules of High-Performance Teamwork*, London: Starting Point, 2020.

D'Amour, Lisa. *Under Pressure: Confronting the Epidemic of Stress and Anxiety in Girls*, New York: Penguin Random House, 2019.

David, Susan. *Emotional Agility: Get Unstuck, Embrace Change, and Thrive in Work and Life*, New York: Avery, 2016.

Duckworth, Angela. *Grit: The Power of Passion and Perseverance*, London: Vermilion, 2016.

Dweck, Carol. *Mindset: The new psychology of success*, New York: Ballantine, 2016.

Eger, Edith. *The Choice: Embrace the Impossible*, London: Rider, 2007.

————. *The Gift: 12 Lessons to Save Your Life*, London: Rider, 2020.

Ferriss, Tim. *The 4-Hour Work Week: Escape the 9-5, Live Anywhere and Join the New Rich*, London: Vermilion, 2008.

Ginnot, Haim. *Teacher and Child: A Book for Parents and Teachers*, New York: Macmillan, 1972.

Goldstuck, Arthur and Nikki Bush. *Tech-savvy Parenting*, Johannesburg: Bookstorm, 2014.

Gratton, Linda and Andrew Scott. *The 100-Year Life: Living and Working in an Age of Longevity*, London: Bloomsbury, 2016.

Harari, Yuval Noah. *Homo Deus: A Brief History of Tomorrow*, New York: Vintage, 2017.

———. *21 Lessons for the 21st Century*, London: Jonathan Cape, 2018.

Kondo, Marie and Scott Sonenshein. *Joy at Work: Organizing Your Professional Life*, New York: Little, Brown Spark, 2020.

Lesser, Elizabeth. *Broken Open: How Difficult Times Help Us Grow*, New York: Villard Books, 2004.

Maxwell, John and Les Parrott. *25 Ways to Win with People: How to Make Others Feel Like a Million Bucks*, Nashville: Nelson Books, 2005.

Phitidis, Pavlo. *Reset, Rebuild, Reignite: Build Your Business to Thrive in a Crisis*, Johannesburg: Pan Macmillan, 2020.

Pink, Daniel H. *Drive: The Surprising Truth About What Motivates Us*, Edinburgh: Canongate Books, 2018.

Rock, David. *Your Brain at Work: Strategies for Overcoming Distraction, Regaining Focus, and Working Smarter All Day Long*, New York: HarperCollins, 2009.

Sefor, Leah. *That's Not What I Meant!*, Cape Town: Tafelberg, 2021.

Semler, Ricardo. *The Seven Day Weekend: Finding the Work/Life Balance*, London: Century, 2003.

Toffler, Alvin. *Future Shock*, New York: Random House, 1970.

Tsabary, Shefali. *The Conscious Parent: Transforming Ourselves, Empowering Our Children*, London: Yellow Kite, 2014.

Verachia, Abdullah. *Disruption Amplified: Reset, Rewire and Reimagine Everything*, Bryanston: Tracey MacDonald Publishers, 2020.

OTHER RESOURCES

Available from the author for download:

- Collateral Damage vs Collateral Beauty exercise: https://nikkibush.com/collateral-damage-vs-collateral-beauty/
- Prioritising exercise template: https://nikkibush.com/download-prioritisation-sheet/
- Reflection and Vision template: https://nikkibush.com/reflection-and-vision/
- Win @ Work and Life Podcast with Nikki Bush: https://nikkibush.podbean.com/

Online resources:

- Garry Landreth's TedX talk, 'Choices, Cookies and Kids', is available at https://www.youtube.com/watch?v=VX1kGm2ousc
- Marcus Buckingham's Standout® Strengths Assessment is available from https://www.marcusbuckingham.com/
- Pomodoro Technique: an introduction to this technique is available at https://lifehacker.com/productivity-101-a-primer-to-the-pomodoro-technique-1598992730
- Susan David's TEDWomen 2017 talk, 'The Gift and Power of Emotional Courage', is available at https://www.youtube.com/watch?v=NDQ1Mi5I4rg; the transcript can be accessed at https://www.ted.com/talks/susan_david_the_gift_and_power_of_emotional_courage/transcript?language=en#t-228903
- The Paradox Mindset Measure from the University of Delaware (udel.edu) is available at http://paradox.lerner.udel.edu
- The World Economic Forum's *The Future of Jobs Report* of October 2020 can be downloaded from http://www3.weforum.org/docs/WEF_Future_of_Jobs_2020.pdf

ABOUT THE AUTHOR

Human-potential and parenting expert Nikki Bush empowers individuals, families and teams in business and education to win at work, home and life. She has the knack of putting difficult, complex and sensitive topics on the table (ones we often prefer to avoid) and making them accessible, such as disruption, loss, adversity, team dynamics, self-leadership, parenting, and much more.

Nikki has written four bestselling parenting books with major publishers, including *Future-proof Your Child for the 2020s and Beyond*, and she has fielded over 3 000 media interviews in the past fifteen years. You may have seen or heard her on her weekly slots on Radio 702 and SABC3's *Expresso*, among many others.

Nikki is a sought-after professional speaker who always speaks with energy, passion, self-deprecating humour and a disarming honesty and vulnerability. She packs a powerful sound bite, whether from the stage or the eighteen different virtual conferencing platforms she has experience with. She has an innate ability to move her audiences as she shares her vivid stories and simple analogies, helping her audience put pictures and words to their own thoughts and feelings. Her audiences are left with valuable insights and practical solutions to help them to win at work and life.

She is a founding member of the Professional Speakers Association of Southern Africa (PSASA), holds the international Certified Speaking Professional (CSP) designation, and was inducted into the Speakers Hall of Fame in 2019 – the first woman in South Africa to ever receive this accolade. She is the 2020/21 president of the Johannesburg chapter of PSASA.

Nikki is the mother of two young men in their twenties. She was married to Simon for twenty-six years before his untimely death in 2017.

For more information and to book Nikki to speak, visit www.nikkibush.com

ENDNOTES

CHAPTER 1

1 Extract from Susan David's TEDWomen 2017 talk, 'The Gift and Power of Emotional Courage', available at https://www.youtube.com/watch?v=NDQ1Mi5I4rg (accessed 15 December 2020)

2 Extract from 'The Gift and Power of Emotional Courage'

3 From https://knowledge.insead.edu/blog/insead-blog/what-will-life-be-like-after-the-pandemic-13886 (accessed 15 December 2020)

CHAPTER 2

4 See https://hbr.org/sponsored/2017/07/digital-transformation-is-racing-ahead-and-no-industry-is-immune-2 (accessed 31 January 2021)

5 Available at https://www.weforum.org/reports/the-future-of-jobs-report-2020 (accessed 21 January 2021)

6 I use the What If™ framework in my work to help individuals and companies anticipate What If™ scenarios and prepare themselves as best they can for them. 'What If "What If™" Happens' is one of my most popular talks. I regularly run educational sessions for large companies, financial advisors and brokers on how to help their clients prepare for What If™ moments or to be more empathetic should a What If™ moment arise.

CHAPTER 3

7 For more information, see https://knowledge.insead.edu/leadership-organisations/overwhelmed-adopt-a-paradox-mindset-14026 (accessed 28 January 2021)

CHAPTER 4

8 For support on family trauma, refer to https://nikkibush.com/help-for-parent-children-families-processing-trauma-covid19/

PART 2: INTRODUCTION

9 From https://globalworkplaceanalytics.com/pros-cons (accessed 26 January 2020)

CHAPTER 6

10 This is from the Vox Telecoms white paper 'Understanding the Intricacies of Working from Home', available from https://www.vox.co.za/content-hub/article/

understanding-the-intricacies-of-working-from-home?page=42171&category=undefined (accessed 15 February 2021)

11 See https://news.stanford.edu/2020/06/29/snapshot-new-working-home-economy/ (accessed 27 January 2021)

12 McKinsey's *Future of Work Report: What's Next for Remote Work* is available at https://www.mckinsey.com/featured-insights/future-of-work/whats-next-for-remote-work-an-analysis-of-2000-tasks-800-jobs-and-nine-countries (accessed 15 February 2021)

13 From https://www.statista.com/statistics/1111316/biggest-struggles-to-remote-work/#:~:text=This%20statistic%20shows%20the%20biggest,and%20communication%20when%20working%20remotely (accessed 21 January 2021)

14 See https://www.theguardian.com/business/2021/jan/13/unilever-workers-will-never-return-to-desks-full-time-says-boss (accessed 19 January 2021)

15 See https://www.itproportal.com/news/jp-morgan-will-adopt-remote-working-on-a-permanent-basis/#:~:text=One%20of%20the%20world's%20largest,to%20the%20office%20full%20time (accessed 1 February 2021)

16 Figures from https://www.flexjobs.com/blog/post/remote-work-statistics/ (accessed 19 January 2021)

17 This information is widely available online; see, for example, https://mariansalzman.com/wp-content/uploads/2020/11/20201119-Trends21-report-final.pdf, and https://www.forbes.com/sites/jackkelly/2019/11/05/microsoft-japan-launched-a-four-day-week-work-to-much-success-is-this-the-answer-to-attract-talent-in-the-tight-us-job-market/?sh=188e469259ff (both accessed 6 January 2021)

CHAPTER 7

18 The 'Keep Your Business Running' white paper can be downloaded from https://nikkibush.com/keep-your-business-running/

19 See https://lifehacker.com/productivity-101-a-primer-to-the-pomodoro-technique-1598992730 (accessed 19 January 2021)

20 'Parenting on the Run' is also the title of a popular parenting workshop I present regularly; more information is available at https://nikkibush.com/parenting-on-run/

CHAPTER 9

21 Elizabeth Lesser, *Broken Open*, pp. 56–66

22 Susan David, 'The Gift and Power of Emotional Courage', https://www.youtube.com/watch?v=NDQ1Mi5I4rg (accessed 15 December 2020)

CHAPTER 12

23 See https://nikkibush.com/children-living-red-zone/

CHAPTER 17

24 Available at www.marcusbuckingham.com (accessed 15 December 2020)

CHAPTER 18

25 Joseph Campbell, *The Power of Myth*, p. 5

26 See www.marcusbuckingham.com (accessed 15 December 2020)

CHAPTER 19

27 See https://www.upwork.com/i/freelance-forward (accessed 28 January 2021)

CHAPTER 23

28 John Maxwell and Les Parrott, *25 Ways to Win with People*, p. 104

29 Ibid., p. 102

30 Caspar Craven, *Be More Human*, p. 39

CHAPTER 24

31 According to Gallup's 'State of the Workplace' report, this figure stands at a low 15 per cent; see https://blog.smarp.com/employee-engagement-8-statistics-you-need-to-know (accessed 28 January 2021)

32 Daniel Pink, *Drive*, p. 111

CHAPTER 25

33 Haim Ginnot, *Teacher and Child*, p. 15

CHAPTER 26

34 Shefali Tsabary, *The Conscious Parent*, p. 11, emphasis in original

CHAPTER 28

35 See https://nikkibush.com/let-go-let-grow/

CHAPTER 30

36 Angela Duckworth, *Grit: the Power of Passion and Perseverance*, p. 169, emphasis in original

ALSO BY NIKKI BUSH: